PANAMA HATS,
CROCODILE TEARS
AND OTHER
COMMON FALLACIES

PANAMA HATS, CROCODILE TEARS AND OTHER COMMON FALLACIES

Philip Ward

BARNES
&NOBLE
BOOKS
NEW YORK

Publisher's Note:

Because Mr. Ward is a native of Great Britain, British spellings
have been used throughout this book, which is an abridged edition
of the original two-volume set titled *A Dictionary of Common
Fallacies*.

Originally published as *A Dictionary of Common Fallacies*
Copyright © 1978, 1980 by Philip Ward and The Oleander Press
Abridged edition © 1993 by Philip Ward and The Oleander Press
All rights reserved.

This edition published by Barnes & Noble, Inc.,
by arrangement with Prometheus Books.

1993 Barnes & Noble Books

ISBN 1-56619-149-1

Printed and bound in the United States of America

M 9 8 7 6 5 4 3 2 1

CONTENTS

PREFACE

The intention of this book is to place before the reader some of the cock-sure but time-worn ideas, cliches and lore once widely held to be true—and often *still* widely held to be so—by sober, decent people. It cannot pretend to be comprehensive, however, because, as the introduction notes, "there is no sign that imposters, charlatans and the plain misguided have diminished in number since the Middle Ages."

Some of the entries may surprise the reader by demonstrating that he or she is the proud possessor of some worthless scrap of misinformation. Do you, for instance, think that the "aisle" is what the bride walks down? Other entries may shock the same reader by dint of *ever* having been believed by anyone at any time: to get your wife to talk in her sleep, place the tongue of a frog over her heart. Still other entries will inspire neither shock nor surprise. They are offered for what they reveal about the anatomy of error itself— how certain ideas came to be enthroned as facts, and how they were eventually and justly deposed. In this sense the book is both a useful reference work and a light-hearted historical one, serving to remind us that the certainties of our own time may very well wind up in similar books in the future.

Of course, if people would rather not find out how much of what they know just isn't so, they can always act like ostriches and bury their heads in the sand. That is, if that's what ostriches really do!

INTRODUCTION

The Lord 'fallere' (to escape from, deceive) gave the Vulgar Latin 'fallire' (to commit a fault, deceive, fail), and the adjective 'fallax' (deceptive), which provided the English adjective fallacious through 'fallaciosus'. In classical logic, a fallacy is understood to denote an argument violating the laws of correct demonstration; more generally, it refers to any mistaken statement used in argument, while in common parlance is understood in the even wider sense of a mistaken view which is held by a relatively large number of people in spite of its having been disproved by some form of scientific or logical test.

The compiler has taken to heart the three mildly sceptical attitudes proposed by Bertrand Russell in *Let the people think:*

(1) That when the experts are agreed, the opposite opinion cannot be held to be certain;
(2) That when they are not agreed, no opinion can be regarded as certain by a non-expert;
(3) That when they all hold that no sufficient grounds for a positive opinion exist, the ordinary man would do well to suspend his judgment.

"These opinions may seem mild", Russell wrote, "yet, if accepted, they would absolutely revolutionize human life. The opinions for which people are willing to fight and persecute all belong to one of the three classes which this scepticism condemns. When there are rational grounds for an opinion, people are content to set forth and wait for them to operate. In such cases, people do not hold their opinions with passion; they hold them calmly, and set forth their reasons quietly. The opinions that are held with passion are always those for which no good ground exists; indeed the passion is the measure of the holder's lack of rational conviction."

There is no sign that impostors, charlatans, and the plain misguided have diminished in numbers since the Middle Ages. The steep rise in population since the Crusades has been accompanied by the fragmentation of a greatly increased quantity of scientific knowledge, so that fewer and fewer possess a clear understanding of a smaller segment of knowledge and their scepticism about their own 'truths', healthy as it is, leaves ample scope for the less scrupulous to protest the truth of new 'religions', occultist movements varying in integrity and intelligence, pseudo-sciences, and obsessions touted as facts.

Excluded from this catalogue of common fallacies are a majority of the phenomena generally classified as *hallucinations and delusions* of an individual or of a closely-knit group which are evidently not shared by the generality of mankind; *hoaxes* except insofar as they have led to fallacious conclusions; mere *ignorance* before major discoveries, inventions, or new patterns of awareness pervade the times; *miracles* of the various churches which have a vested interest in advertising the power of their magic or the ease with which they can obtain favours from a deity; simple *mistakes* which are subsequently recognized and rectified; *occult* beliefs, which appeal, however irrationally, to a sector of the consciousness allegedly different from that to which known scientific principles can be seen to apply; *religious systems* which, through their dogma of faith, claim to be immune from the process of verification which is logically applicable to them as to everything else; *superstitions*, which are by their nature irrational and, as their name suggests, constitute survivals of religious systems now aban-

x

doned; and *unsolved mysteries,* which are stated with data that are normally either incomplete or prejudiced.

One final note: describing an idea as a 'common fallacy' does not of course thereby automatically make it so; the intention is merely to reflect the best opinion currently available and the reader's indulgence is craved for mistakes and distortions which, regrettably, as the book demonstrates, are all too obviously part of the human condition.

A

Athens has the Only **Acropolis**

Many Greek cities, whether on the mainland of Greece and Asia Minor, or on the islands, had an *akropolis*, largely for purposes of military defence. One thinks of Tiryns on the mainland, say, or Lindos on Rhodes. *Akros* is the Greek for 'topmost, highest', and *polis* means 'city', so the akropolis is that upper city which is most easily defended against a besieging force. The example at Athens is merely the best-known of hundreds.

Human Beings Can Live to a Great **Age**

Every two or three years there is an excited press comment somewhere in the world, usually from Georgia or Azerbaijan in the Soviet Union, or from a South American 'lost valley' in Ecuador, Colombia, or Bolivia, that a race of men has lived to fantastic ages: anywhere from 130 to 180 in some cases. Solemn interviews are reported, during which the recipe for long life is variously stated: 'an outdoor existence', 'a wholly milk-related diet', 'pure air and vigorous daily exercise', and 'abstinence from smoking' are some of the most common.

The curious common factor in these reports is the absence of a proportionate number of elders between 70 and 90 years of age. The facts are that no birth records are maintained for those individuals; great age is venerated so it is in one's interest to exaggerate it; they are illiterate or semi-literate with no accurate idea of time; and (in the case of Soviet citizens) many males added years to their age to avoid military service under the Tsar and induced their wives to do likewise.

No genuine case is recorded so far of a person older than 114 years.

Brides Walk Up the **Aisle**

Not unless they lose their way they don't. 'Aisle' (from the French *aile*, wing) is one of the lateral passages of a church. The bride walks along the central passage.

King **Alfred** Burnt the Cakes, Disguised Himself as a Minstrel and Founded the University of Oxford

Alfred (849–901) was too practical to allow his supper to be burnt on the hearth, too wary to go masquerading as a minstrel in the Danish camp, and the first note of students at Oxford occurs in the 12th century. Three fallacies out of three. The legends which gathered around the names of Theseus, Alexander the Great, Roland, and King Arthur, have suffered similar nationalistic and mystic accretions which obscure serious archaeology and historical explanation.

About 1600 a forger interpolated into Asser's *Life of King Alfred* a statement dating to 877 the destruction of a large Danish fleet off Swanage. It was only in Stevenson's edition of Asser (1912) that the forged paragraphs were clearly shown to be interpolated.

That by *Algebra* One Can Make Two Equal One

The notion has been current since George Bernard Shaw first admitted to being hoodwinked by a schoolboy friend.

Mr Shaw's youthful experience about x and a are so highly instructive that I cannot refrain from dwelling upon them for a moment. His friend induced him to "let $x=a$" and Mr Shaw—not expecting that x would take any mean advantage of the permission—granted the request. But he did not understand that in letting $x=a$ he was also letting $xt-a=0$, and the proof (of the proposition, 2=1) that "followed with rigorous exactness," assumed that $x-a$ did *not* equal 0.

Any *Angle* Can be Trisected

Several thousand mathematicians—most of them amateur—have proved to their own satisfaction (though they have rarely convinced anyone else) that any angle can be trisected. After all, it is simple to bisect an angle, and to divide a line segment into any number of equal parts. It is easy to trisect a right angle of 180°, and—by bisecting the 30° angle—the 45° angle. Many special angles can be trisected, but a general method which can be applied to any angle is impossible. The rigorous proof was first supplied by P. L. Wantzel in 1837, and is expounded for the curious non-mathematician by Richard Courant and Herbert Robbins in their *What is mathematics?*

The impossibility of trisecting an angle has not stopped a small army from wasting their time: one thinks of William Upton's *Geometry versus algebra; or the trisection of an angle geometrically solved* (The Author, Bath, *c.* 1849); James Sabben's *A method to trisect a series of angles having relation to each other; also another to trisect any given angle* (2 pages, 1848); the Very Reverend Jeremiah Joseph Callahan's *The trisection of the angle* (Pittsburgh, 1931); and of Maurice Kidjel of Honolulu, whose book—written with K. W. K. Young—called *The two hours that shook the world* claimed not only to trisect the angle but also to square the circle and to duplicate the cube!

Deryagin and **Anomalous Water**

In the early 1960s, a Russian physical chemist called Boris Deryagin reported to a puzzled scientific press certain unusual phenomena in water condensed from the vapour in fine glass capillaries. His view that the compound H_2O has more than one liquid form was apparently confirmed by the strange behaviour on melting, unusual Raman spectrum, and high viscosity. Hundreds of detailed experiments were carried out in the U.S.A., the U.S.S.R. and elsewhere to explore this discovery; it was argued that it must be a polymer of ordinary water and was accordingly called 'polywater'.

However, there is no such thing as 'anomalous water' or 'polywater'. The anomalous properties of the condensate must have been due to a number of chemical impurities dissolved from the glass: one such impurity was human sweat!

5

The **Ant** and the Grasshopper

An inconvenience of animal fables is that they are often based on a fallacy: none more so than this. The ant is supposed to labour all summer to provide for the winter. But the harvester ants which do in fact lay up stocks are uncommon. Most ants live on food that could not be stored anyway, but they wouldn't need it even if it could, for they are usually torpid in winter.

The grasshopper, alleged to beg from the ant, does no such thing: the ant steals from the grasshopper.

Antimony or 'Monk's Bane' was So Called Because it Poisoned Monks

There is an entertaining fallacy concerned with the folk etymology of *antimoine*, the French for 'antimony', 'moine' denoting a monk. The legend goes that the Benedictine monk Valentinus of Erfurt, author of the *Currus triumphalis antimonii* first published in 1624 and translated into English as *Basil Valentine his triumphant chariot of antimony* (London, 1678), discovered common antimony. He found that the pigs in his monastery enjoyed the plant, and so fed it to his brethren, who expired. The plant was then said to be 'anti-monk'.

Nobody knows the true origin of the name. The best guess of the *Oxford English Dictionary* derives the word from the distant Arabic *uthmud*, but the fact is that we simply don't know.

Green **Apples** Will Give You Indigestion

Anything will give you indigestion if eaten too quickly. The fallacy about eating unripe apples probably arose from the greed of little boys who stole the apples before they were mature, straight from the tree, and gobbled them down quickly because they were afraid of being caught and, since it was not yet the apple season, they were avid for apples.

The real cause of their indigestion was the haste with which the food was eaten. Dr. August A. Thomen assures us, in *Doctors don't believe it: why should you?* (New York, 1935), "If an apple is eaten slowly, and sufficiently chewed, the stomach cannot distinguish between a ripe and an unripe one".

The **Arctic** Is an Area of Eternal Snow and Unendurable Cold

These popular errors stem from an ignorant assumption that cold increases in close proportion to distance north (or south) of the Equator. But more snow falls in Virginia, U.S.A., than in the Arctic lowlands. Reykjavik, Iceland's capital, is only just below the Arctic Circle, but its mean annual temperature is actually higher than that of New York City. Montana has recorded a temperature 10° Fahrenheit colder than the North Pole's record.

Aristotle Committed Suicide By Drowning

One of the two greatest philosophers that classical Greek civilization produced, Aristotle, died in the year 322 B.C., a year after the death of Alexander (one of his pupils) and of his own retirement to Euboea. His *Prior and posterior analytics* ('analytics' being his word for what we know as logic), written probably between 350 and 344, are still available in a handy edition and translation by John Warrington (London, 1964), who has called the book "one of the greatest achievements of the human intellect; [it] served for more than two thousand years as the controlling instrument of western thought in every department of knowledge, human and divine".

There is absolutely no reason for thinking that Aristotle died any other than a natural death according to Ingemar Düring, but Procopius, Justin Martyr and others passed on the mistaken belief that Aristotle drowned himself in the narrow strait of Euripus, separating Boeotia from Euboea by only forty metres or so near the town of Chalkis.

Let the inimitable Sir Thomas Browne take up the story: "That Aristotle drowned himselfe in Euripus as despairing to resolve the cause of its reciprocation, or ebbe and flow seven times a day, with this determination, *Si quidem ego non capio te tu capies me* ['If I don't understand *(lit.* 'seize') you, you will seize me'], was the assertion of Procopius, Nazianzen, Iustine Martyr, and is generally beleeved amongst us; wherein, because we perceive men have but an imperfect knowledge, some conceiving Euripus to be a River, others not knowing where or in what part to place it . . ."

Auburn *Originally Meant Reddish-Brown*

The Latin 'alburnus' (whitish, nearly white) passed through many forms in English, from the Old French 'alborne, auborne', to reach its present spelling.

It was as late as the 16th century that we find the common forms like 'abroun' which induced many English-speakers to compare and even to derive the word from the root for 'brown', and thus pervert the original meaning of a colour related to white to that of a colour related to brown.

By the time we come to Scott's *Marmion* (1808), the poet can write (v., ix): "And auburn of the darkest dye, His short curled beard and hair . . ."

B

The **Bagpipe** Is a Scottish Instrument

An instrument of great antiquity, known to the ancient Greeks as the *askaulos* or *symphoneia,* and to the Romans as *tibia utricularis.* It is the French *cornemuse,* the Italian *cornamusa,* and the German *Sackpfeife.* The bagpipe appears on a coin of Nero's time and Nero himself is reputed (by Suetonius and Dion Chrysostomos) to have played it. Chaucer's miller performed on it: "A bagpipe well couth he blowe and sowne". The Highland bagpipe is just one of a hundred variants.

There Is a **Balcony** Scene in *Shakespeare's* Romeo and Juliet

Shakespeare's so-called 'Balcony Scene' in *Romeo and Juliet* was probably known to him and his fellow-actors and audience as the 'Orchard Scene' or the 'Gallery Scene' for the word balcony was imported from Italy *(balcone,* a gallery) later in the 17th century. Incidentally, the stress was, as usual in Italian, on the penultimate syllable (as in Marconi), and the 19th-century writer Samuel Rogers complained that " 'cóntemplate' is bad enough, but 'bálcony' makes me sick".

A **Banister** Is a Handrail on a Staircase

The whole construction protecting those on an upper floor from falling is a *balustrade.* A banister is one of the bars running from the handrail to the steps. A stone balustrade's bars are more accurately termed balusters or colonets.

Baseball Was First Played in the U.S.A.

The first game of baseball played under the Cartwright rules was played at Hoboken (New Jersey) on 19 June 1846, but there is a woodcut of "Base-Ball" printed in England as early as 1744, and the Russians too claim to have preceded Americans in playing the game. The 'Baseball Ground' in Derby was the scene of experimental baseball games in Britain, but the sport never became popular, and from 1895 the ground has been the home of Derby County Football Club, founded in 1884 and one of the original members of the Football League.

Bats and *Moles Are* Blind

Bats are not blind, but as they have evolved as nocturnal hunters they can see better in half-light than in the full light of day. 'Blind as a mole' is equally fallacious, since though their eyes are very small (like the eyes of other creatures that burrow underground), moles are perfectly capable of seeing.

The *Bayeux Tapestry* Is a Tapestry
Made at Bayeux

The 'Bayeux tapestry' is not a tapestry at all, but a long embroidered hanging worked in coloured wools on a plain background of bleached linen. It was commissioned by the half-brother of William the Conqueror, Bishop Odo of Bayeux (hence the designation), but it was made, between about 1067 and 1070, in England (where Odo was residing at the time), and not in France, as is commonly supposed.

Signs to the 'tapestry' in Bayeux today are to 'La tapisserie de la Reine Mathilde', crediting William's wife Mathilde with the embroidery, an attribution discredited today by all French historians.

Bears Hug Their Victims to Death

There have been very few instances of an unprovoked attack by a polar bear or grizzly bear on a human being (they avoid man whenever possible), but those attacks that are recorded give no support whatsoever to the common fallacy that bears hug or squeeze their victims. Neither do they generally eat their victims (though they will eat much else, down to insects).

Bears kill large victims with a single blow of a forepaw, which is known to be strong enough to break the neck of a large bison.

Dates *'Before Christ'* and *'Anno Domini'* Have Long Been Used

We began to think in terms of years 'in the year of our Lord' *(Anno Domini)* in Christian Europe as late as A.D. 525, taking up the suggestion of that year from Dionysius Exiguus.

However, years 'Before Christ' were only cited thus as recently as the 17th century, and the first to have used it may have been Jacques-Bénigne Bossuet (1627–1704) in his *Discours sur l'histoire universelle* (Paris, 1681). Bossuet's work is the last in the long series of world histories leading from the Creation by God to the divine choice of the writer's homeland as the culmination of the historical process, a tendency leading to feudal ideas, caste or class divisions, extreme patriotism, and theocentric absolutism. Bossuet was duly rewarded with a bishopric and the lavish rewards of Louis XIV. Voltaire refuted Bossuet's errors in his *Essai sur l'histoire générale et sur les moeurs et l'esprit des nations* (Geneva, 1756), which rejected biblical teleology in favour of a philosophical approach to history, and began the modern school of comparative historiography which replaces divine guidance and Eurocentrism with scientific explanations based on observation and the inclusion of other continents, and other ways of life than those immediately familiar to the writer.

Bell-Ringing *Can Save Cities from Lightning*

The Middle Ages in Europe was a period when it was almost ubiquitously believed that the ringing of church bells would diminish the damage done by storms, and even prevent lightning.

Descartes (in *De meteoribus*) and Francis Bacon (in his *Natural history*) both refer to the belief with respect as late as the 17th century, suggesting that the bells may fulfil this function by their concussion of the air!

The main written source of the fallacy is *De gentibus septentrionalibus* (Rome, 1555) by the Primate of Sweden, Olaus Magnus, who declares it a well-established fact that cities and harvests may be saved from lightning by the ringing of bells, and incidentally also by the burning of consecrated incense, accompanied by prayers. The fact that nobody ever reported a case when lightning had *not* been stopped by such measures does not mean that there were no such cases!

'Between' Is Correctly Used of Two, and 'Among' of More Than Two

I suppose most of us were taught that it is wrong to say 'there was a discussion between the five of us', but the standard *Oxford English Dictionary* states that from the earliest appearance of the word it has been "extended to more than two"; Fowler concurs, as do Merriam Webster's 3rd edition and Theodore M. Bernstein in *The careful writer* (New York, 1965). Bernstein adds, "To speak of a treaty *between* nine powers would be completely proper and exact".

Birds *Sleep With Their Heads*
Under Their Wings

A fallacy which gave rise to a popular nursery rhyme and has in turn been reinforced by the rhyme:

"The north wind doth blow,
    and we shall have snow;
And what will Cock Robin do then, poor thing?
    He'll fly to the barn,
    To keep himself warm,
And hide his head under his wing, poor thing".

A bird's method of going to sleep can be roughly described as turning its head round, putting it on its back with the beak concealed, and often in the process almost concealing the head, but never in any case so far recorded placing the head under the wings.

It is Possible to Travel in Space
Through **'Black Holes'**

Adrian Berry, in *The iron sun: crossing the universe through black holes* (London, 1977), fallaciously argues that travel through collapsars (as the Russians call 'black holes') is technically feasible. A black hole, however, is definable as a region in space from which nothing (not even light) can escape against the pull of gravity; it is probably the end of the life-cycle of a large star. Berry suggests that the traveller will arrive at another part of the universe through entering a 'black hole' but this view is contradicted by the current definition, according to which nothing (not even the optimistic traveller) can escape. In his detailed criticism of Berry's thesis, Derek Raine in *The Times Literary Supplement* for 29 July 1977 concludes that: "If this book were intended merely as commercially oriented light entertainment (or as a hoax), so be it. But what is claimed, amid learned references and explanatory appendixes, is that the light-barrier has been *shown* to be mythical. Sadly, for those who like their fantasies to be laced with a drop of reality, this claim has simply not been substantiated".

Bligh of the Bounty
Was a Tyrannical Captain

We are all indebted to Gavin Kennedy for refuting the above fallacy with unquestionable documentation in his book *Bligh* (London, 1978). The mutiny on the 'Bounty' which took place on 28 April 1789 resulted not so much from any failure on the part of William Bligh, a commander who had learnt his seamanship under Captain Cook, as to serious overcrowding on the 215-ton 'Bounty', a shortage of proven men, and the mental breakdown of Fletcher Christian.

Christian's collapse was due not to persecution by Captain Bligh, according to the evidence now adduced by Dr Kennedy, of the University of Strathclyde, but to his own mental instability. Christian talked of taking a raft through a shark-infested sea to a shore thirty miles away, and "had tied a heavy weight round his neck to bring a speedy end to his life if the mutiny failed and he had to jump over the side". Dr Kennedy indicates the ways in which Christian's powerful family tried to exculpate Christian by defaming Bligh, and how most subsequent writers on Bligh "accepted the partisan rumour-mongering of the mutineers and other survivors". The mutiny is attributed to Christian's resentment after Bligh had pointed out the inadequacy of Christian's performance as acting lieutenant. Christian had an instinct to run from trouble instead of controlling it, resorted to unnecessary violence, and treated the Tahitians in an "appalling" manner.

Boomerangs Are Used Because *They Return to the Thrower*

The great majority of boomerangs, used predominantly by Australian aborigines in war and hunting, will not return and are not intended to do so. The returning boomerang is completely unknown in Central Australia and Northern Territory. It is used in tests of skill, and its main use is in throwing *above* flights of duck, which mistake it for a hovering hawk and consequently fly low into nets placed by the aborigines.

Lucrezia **Borgia** *Was a Woman of Unparalleled Evil*

Ferdinand Gregorovius, in his *Lucrezia Borgia* (London, 1948, following the German edition of Stuttgart, 1874), states: "Among Lucrezia's accusers only those who were actual witnesses of her life in Rome are worthy of attention; and Guicciardini, her bitterest enemy, is not of this number. The verdicts of all later writers, however, have been based upon his opinion of Lucrezia, because of his fame as a statesman and historian. He himself made up his estimate from current gossip or from the satires of Pontanus and Sannazzaro —two poets who lived in Naples and not in Rome. Their epigrams merely show that they were inspired by a deep-seated hatred of Alexander and Cesare, who had wrought the overthrow of the Aragonese dynasty, and further with what crimes men were to credit evil-doers".

William Roscoe was the first to question Guicciardini's conclusions, offering in her favour the evidence of her later life at Ferrara, which was exemplary, according to Roscoe, in its domesticity. Roscoe's version was amplified by William Gilbert (father of W. S. Gilbert, of Gilbert and Sullivan) in *Lucrezia Borgia* (2 vols., London, 1869), who cites Lucrezia's own letters as [surely a rather dubious] testimony to the faithfulness with which she carried out her domestic duties. Gilbert acknowledges the unlikelihood of her residing for some twenty years in the foul atmosphere of her father's court in Rome without having been contaminated by it at least in some degree, but asserts that her detractors are too vocal in their denunciation.

Gregorovius absolves Lucrezia from the charge of complicity in the murder of her second husband, Alfonso di Bisceglia, and discredits the accusations of incest, citing the divorced Giovanni Sforza's motive to retaliate on the family which had discarded and disinherited him. Let Gregorovius be heard, too, on the fallacy of any sweeping, over-confident judgment of such historical figures as Lucrezia: "Men of past ages are

20

merely problems which we endeavour to solve. If we err in our conception of our contemporaries, how much more likely are we to be wrong when we endeavour to analyse men whose very forms are shadowy. All the circumstances of their personal life, of their nature, the times, and their environment—of which they were the product—all the secrets of their being exist only as disconnected fragments from which we are forced to frame our conception of their characters. History is merely a world-judgment based upon the law of causality".

Incidentally, it is also a fallacy that 'Borgia' is the original name of the family: it was Spanish, and Borgia is merely the closest that the Italians could come to the pronunciation of Borja, their true name.

Robert the **Bruce** Was a Scotsman

Robert de Bruis (1274–1329) may have been King of Scotland, but he belonged to a Norman family which landed with William the Conqueror in 1066. A good French aristocrat.

Bulls are Infuriated by the Colour Red

No: bulls are infuriated by a cruel posturing mercenary 'fighter' waving a cloth in front of him to the accompaniment of merciless cheering by bloodthirsty spectators. Bulls cannot distinguish red from any other colour, and *matadores* who experimentally used white capes in their antics produced an identical reaction. While visiting Palma de Mallorca in 1976 I found a poster advertising bloodless bullfights for the benefit of squeamish tourists, and Portuguese bullfights are traditionally bloodless. The colour red was probably first used partly because in strong sunlight it is the most brilliant colour, and partly because it does not show blood so clearly.

Cows Which Eat **Buttercups**
Give the Yellowest Butter

A folk fallacy found in several parts of the British Isles. Buttercups grow only on good pastureland, the surrounding grass of which is likely to improve butter (and milk) quality by giving the best quality feed to the cow. Cows will not eat the buttercups, a noxious, bitter weed.

C

The **Caesarean Section** was First Performed at the Birth of Julius Caesar

The Caesarean section, in earlier times, involved saving the life of a newborn child at the expense of its mother by removing the child through a cut made in the front of the abdomen. The operation, known as Caesarean section, is popularly believed to have been first performed on Julia, mother of Julius Caesar, but the operation is not recorded as early as 100 B.C., and Julia lived many years after the birth of the future Dictator.

The name 'Caesarean section' probably derives from the so-called 'Lex Regia' or 'Lex Caesarea', which decreed that the child should be removed from every woman who died when far advanced in pregnancy, even in cases where the child stood no chance of survival, so that mother and child might be buried separately. Such a case is obviously inapplicable to Julia and her son.

Incidentally, Caesar was never Roman Emperor (there was no 'Empire' as such until after his time), but first Consul (five times) and eventually Dictator.

Camelhair Brushes are Made from the Hair of Camels

Camelhair brushes are made for artists and architects from the hair of the tails of Russian squirrels. The hair of camels, on the other hand, was used for making carpets, tent-cloths, and for mixing with silk. But the advent of synthetic fibres has vastly reduced the use of the hair of camels, as well as that of 'camelhair'.

24

Camels Have a Hump for Storing Water

Camels have a hump (or two humps in the case of a Bactrian) which does *not* have a hollow reservoir for water inside. Excess food and drink that the camel does not need at once are stored in the body as fat and other substances, to be drawn on in time of need. Water is present not only in the hump (together with the fat) but is stored also in other body tissues and in the stomach pouches, allowing the animal to survive without drinking for seven days (if working quite actively) or ten to twelve days (if inactive).

Canary Birds Gave Their Name to the Canary Islands

Quite the reverse! The Latin name *insula Canaria* derived from the large *canes* or dogs found there. Birds exported from these islands off the western coast of Morocco were called 'canaries' from the place they came from, not the other way round.

Cat Fallacies

In the U.S.A., Spain, and some other countries, a white cat is considered lucky, and a black cat unlucky. In Britain, the opposite fallacy prevails. Neither has of course a grain of truth in it. Both go back to the time when 'witches' were assumed to have 'familiars' and most old ladies living alone kept a cat for company, so the 'familiar' must have been a cat. A black cat's green eyes, seen apparently 'disembodied' in the dark, have been a source of fear to the ignorant and nervous.

Charles Darwin, no less, wrote in *The descent of man* that "the tortoise-shell colour, which is confined to female cats, is quite distinct at birth". But Kit Wilson's *Cat encyclopedia* (Kingswood, Surrey, 1951) disagrees. "There have been statements that sexual difference of colouring has been found in the cat tribe. This is a fallacy, and probably arose over the question of the red male being the counterpart of the tortoiseshell female. This theory has been exploded very successfully; there are as many red females on the show bench today as males, also some tortoiseshell males have made their appearance".

Cats can see in the dark, but *only* if the dark is not complete. In pitch blackness, the cat is as helpless as you or I.

It is also a fallacy that 'pedigree' cats are of outstanding quality. In *Cats* (Harmondsworth, 1957), Brian Vesey-Fitzgerald observes: "It should be pointed out that *every* cat, that every living creature, has a pedigree. It may not always be known, and it may be very disreputable, but it is a pedigree. What is meant by the term 'pedigree cat' is a cat whose ancestry on both sides is known for some generations back, a cat with the unadulterated blood of a particular breed. This does not necessarily mean that it is a cat of outstanding quality. No breeder can say what qualities are going to appear in the kittens of any particular mating".

The cat's sense of smell is commonly thought to be poor. "Indeed", writes Vesey-Fitzgerald, "you do sometimes meet people who maintain that the cat has no sense of smell. In fact, the cat has an exceptionally acute and delicate sense of smell—much more delicate than has the dog".

26

The cat's tail is usually regarded as a balancing organ. But Manx cats, which are tailless, are just as good at balancing as tailed cats.

Catgut

Catgut is not that at all, but the fibrous layer of sheep's intestine, toughened with chromic acid. The strings of musical instruments owe nothing whatsoever to the domestic cat.

The Year Ending 31 December 2000 Is the First Year of a **Century**

The year beginning 1 January 2000 and ending on 31 December 2000 is the last year of the 20th century, not the first year of the 21st. The reason is that the Christian calendar dates from 1 January of the year 1, not the year 0.

Chameleons Match Their Background

Most people would swear that this is the case, though few of them have seen a chameleon. In fact, though experiments have proved that many of these lizards can indeed change colour rapidly, there is no evidence that the colour of their background has any but a marginal importance, the main factors influencing colour change being light, temperature, and the chameleon's health and feelings. (Human beings also change colour within a limited range according to their feelings, though not as violently as the terms 'purple', 'white' or 'red' would indicate).

Those keeping a chameleon are advised not to take too seriously the fallacy perpetuated by Shakespeare in *Hamlet* (III, ii, 98) that the reptile lives on air.

The *'Charge'* was Sounded at Balaclava

Contrary to the accepted story, the 'Charge' was never sounded at Balaclava. Nor did Lord Cardigan, once his brigade was in motion, by trumpet, voice, or signal, issue any command.

Weak **Chins** Signify Weak Personalities

It is a mystery how the 'chinless wonder' myth arose to scoff at the ineffectual English upper-class dolt celebrated in the stories and novels of P. G. Wodehouse, among others.

Frederick the Great, General Wolfe, and Queen Victoria had receding chins, but nobody has yet had the temerity (or the ignorance) to call them weak characters.

This fallacy is one of the class deriving from the erroneous supposition that one can tell a person's character by looking.

Of the three hundred or so early versions of this popular fairy tale (including a Chinese story of the 9th century), not one described Cinderella's slippers as made
of glass, because they weren't. The mediaeval French
version used by Perrault (1628–1703), author of the
Cinderella we know today, described the slippers as
'pantoufles en vair', or slippers of white ermine. Perrault remembered the word as 'verre', or glass, and
thus it has erroneously been ever since.

Scottish Highland **Clans** *Comprised*
A Chief and His Followers,
Who All Bore His Name
and Were Related to Him
by Ties of Blood

This fallacy has been refuted by a study of rentals and
similar documents such as Exchequer Rolls and Forfeited Estates Papers.

It can be proved that there could not have been any
blood tie between the first chief of such clans as the
Bissets, Chisholms, Grants and Frasers, whose chiefs
were originally Norman. In fact, however, the same is
true in the case of clan chiefs of purely Scottish origin.
A Highland rental of 1505 (for Kintyre) shows a large
number of surnames borne by long-term tenants on
the estates of Macdonald, the clan chief. Similar pictures are presented by estates such as Lochiel and
Clanranald which were forfeited after Culloden. Gregory, in *Collectanea de rebus albanicis* (published by
the Iona Club), showed that these tenants were repre-

sentatives of families which had been on the lands in question from long before, under a succession of different, and unrelated, chiefs. "They were not, nor did they claim to be, of the blood of the individual whom they acknowledged to be their chief. They appear to have formed the bulk of the population of the Highlands". Gregory amplifies the point by citing the case of the Stewart followers, 69 of whom were killed at Culloden, and a further 40 of whom were wounded. Between them, these followers bore 18 different surnames, none of them Stewart.

The word 'clan' has been understood in three different senses: the narrowest indicates the family of the chief himself; the next circle consists of families descended from that of the chief; the widest sense include followers lacking any kinship with the chief and his family. The third class has been called 'septs', but it is now clear that the term 'septs' (roughly 'divisions') ought to be applied instead to the second class, and the term 'followers' or 'tenants' would more helpfully describe the third class.

Cleopatra Was an Egyptian

Cleopatra (68–30 B.C.) was the eldest daughter of Ptolemy XI, the illegitimate son of Ptolemy VIII, son of Ptolemy VII. The Ptolemies were a Greek dynasty, and Cleopatra was Greek.

The granite obelisks known as Cleopatra's Needles have nothing whatsoever to do with her, but were erected at Heliopolis by Thothmes III about 1600 B.C. The 'Cleopatra's Needle' on the Embankment in London was brought to England in 1878.

Feed a **Cold** and Starve a Fever

The implication of this ancient, universal saw is that patients with colds must be given a great deal to eat, and those fevers very little. This is nonsense.

The original meaning might have been more intelligible as 'If you give too much food to a patient with a cold, he will then contract a fever, during which he will not desire to eat'. That is, that one must *not* give patients with colds a great deal to eat. This too is nonsense, for there is no known correlation between cold cure and the consumption of food. Those with a bad cold often have a fever too.

Patients with a cold normally require no more food than when they are in normal health, and no less. Patients in the early stages of fever will have little desire to eat, and in the later stages they will require extra food to make up their previous loss.

Christians were Thrown to the Lions at the **Colosseum**, Rome

George Bernard Shaw's *Androcles and the Lion* is only one of the multitude of antihistorical books, plays and films that have perpetuated this ancient error, which seems to have been due to a desire to manufacture martyrs in Rome (another case is the Catacombs fraud). No Christian was ever exposed to the lions or to any other sort of death in the Roman Colosseum.

The **Colour-Blind** Can See Only Grey

This is undoubtedly true of the most extreme cases, but much more frequently the blindness applies to only one colour or two. Most colour blindness seems to apply to green, and less to red, while some of those who are colour-blind confuse green and red. The colour-blind are otherwise good at matching colours and tend to have normal vision in all else. About one man in twenty-five is colour-blind, but only about one woman in 250.

Machines are More Sensitive to **Colour** than are Men and Women

The most accurate photo-electric spectro-photometers can detect no more than 5,000,000 different colours.

The unaided human eye, in the best possible conditions, can distinguish as many as 10,000,000 different colours.

Columbus Intended to Land in America

Columbus had no inkling of the existence of the American continent, and failed to discover *India*. "The Columbian tradition, transmitted through Columbus' son Fernando and his historian Las Casas, has given to later generations a picture of the Discoverer struggling for a new idea against entrenched unscientific conservatism. This representation of Columbus' scientific activity is certainly false; the more enlightened his critics were in the science of their day, the more firmly would they have to reject his ridiculous scientific ideas."

The Husband of a Countess Is a **Count**

In French, a *comtesse* is the wife of a *comte*, and in Italian, a *contessa* is the wife of a *conte*. But in English, a countess is the wife not of a count, but of an earl, from the Anglo-Saxon *eorl* (a warrior). The word 'count' (originally Lat. *comes*, Acc. *comitem* meant 'companion') eventually became a military title, as in *Comes littoris Saxonici* (Count of the Saxon Coast), the Roman general responsible for the southeastern coastline of Britain.

Crocodiles Shed Tears of Remorse

Pliny's colourful account of the crocodile in the *Historia naturalis* is as full of fallacies as Seneca's in the *Naturales quaestiones*. Most classical authors thought that 'crocodile tears' were false tears indicating hypocritical remorse: Aelius Spartianus *(c.* A.D. 300) indicated that these were the kind of tears that Caracalla shed. As recently as 1642, Sir John Suckling (who invented the game of cribbage) could write "She's false, false as the tears of crocodiles" in his play *The Sad One* (Act IV, sc. 5).

But as usual Lewis Carroll was nearer the truth when, in *Alice's Adventures in Wonderland* (how many readers commit the fallacy of miscalling the novel *Alice in Wonderland?*), he wrote in parody:

"How doth the little crocodile
    Improve his shining tail,
And pour the waters of the Nile
    On every golden scale!

How cheerfully he seems to grin,
    How neatly spread his claws,
And welcomes little fishes in
    With gently smiling jaws!"

Note the *little* fish. The operative word is 'little', for when it is champing great lumps of meat and only then does the crocodile shed the tears in question. Let L. J. and Margery Milne take up the story in *The balance of nature* (New York, 1960, p. 57): "While it breaks up its larger victims into pieces before trying to swallow them, it gulps larger food-chunks than it can easily manage. When a large chunk goes down often the crocodile gasps for air . . . and at these times its tear glands discharge copiously".

Using a **Cross** as Signature
Indicates Illiteracy

For many centuries men of learning in Europe made the cross as the traditional way of *signing* their name, even though they could of course have spelt out their name had they wanted to do so. But the spelling out of the name was normally done by a witness to authenticate the sign. In the 17th century, certain educated people felt distaste at using the sign of the cross for secular or even mercantile purposes, and used instead their initials or some other sign recognized as their own.

Curse of the Pharaohs

Lord Carnarvon, who financed the excavation of the Tomb of Tut-Ankh-Amun in Egypt, died six weeks after his visit to the tomb of a mosquito bite. Howard Carter, who discovered the tomb also died—seventeen years later. The joke about the 'Curse of the Pharaohs' which took in so many people in 1922, when the tomb was first opened, was started by the Egyptologist Arthur Weigall as a hoax. It is not at all remarkable that ten people connected in some way with the Tut-Ankh-Amun expedition died within ten years. Richard Adamson, a survivor, expressed his disbelief in the curse on television in 1971.

This hoax became a fallacy because it was so tenacious in the popular mind that when a director of the Cairo Museum, Dr Mehrez, died in the early 1970s, his death was connected with the 'curse'.

D

Dante Called His Comedy 'Divine'

Dante Alighieri wrote his great trilogy as *La Commedia* (as opposed to a 'tragedy') in the early 14th century, but it was not printed until 1472, at Foligno. The Botticelli drawings probably commissioned by Lorenzo de' Medici inspired a remarkable series of engravings by Baldini first published in 1481. The epithet 'divina' was coined neither by Dante himself nor by any of his contemporaries, but appeared first on the title-page of Lodovico Dolci's edition of the great poem dated 1555.

No Life Exists in the **Dead Sea**

But it does. Micro-organisms were reported to exist in the Dead Sea in *Nature* (12 September 1936, p. 467). The old tale that 'Birds will not fly over the Dead Sea' has also been exploded by eyewitnesses.

More Fallacies on the **Dead Sea**

The major source of Dead Sea fallacies is Andrew D. White's *A history of the warfare of science with theology in Christendom* (London, 1955, 2 vols. in 1, vol. 2, pp. 209 ff.). Dr White deals with the curious fallacy of Lot's wife turned into a pillar of salt (there are analogous false explanations for curious natural phenomena in all other religions and mythologies); the foul smells of the area attributed to supernatural causes (actually caused by sulphur in mineral springs); the error that "the very beautiful apples" that grow there will "burn and are reduced to ashes and smoke as if they are still burning"; the notion that the Dead Sea is the mouth of Hell (due to the hot springs in the area); and the hoary errors repeated in Sir John Mandeville's *Travels* that "if a man cast iron therein, it will float above. And if men cast a feather therein, it will sink to the bottom, and these be things against kind".

White continues: "In the fifteenth century wonders increased. In 1418 we have the Lord of Caumont, who makes a pilgrimage and gives us a statement which is the result of the theological reasoning of centuries, and especially interesting as a typical example of the theological method in contrast with the scientific. He could not understand how the blessed waters of the Jordan could be allowed to mingle with the accursed waters of the Dead Sea. In spite, then, of the eye of sense, he beheld the water with the eye of faith, and calmly announced that the Jordan water passes through the sea, but that the two masses of water are not mingled".

The great works on the theological necessity for turning Lot's wife into salt are Franciscus Quaresmius of Lodi's *Historica, theologica et moralis Terrae Sanctae elucidatio* (2 vols., Antwerp, 1631), and *De uxore Lothi in statuam salis conversa* (Copenhagen, 1720) by the theologian Masius. The latter scholar comes to the apparently ingenious conclusion that Lot's wife must have been turned into a pillar of salt, because many travellers have seen a pillar of salt and the positive testimony of those who have seen it must outweigh the negative testimony of those who have not!

There are *nineteen* more pages devoted to fallacies concerning the Dead Sea in Andrew White's fascinating compendium, to which readers are referred.

Fallacies Concerning **Deafness**
and the Deaf

1. *'Deaf and dumb'* (a term now frowned upon because it is so open to misinterpretation): 'dumb' does *not* imply 'unable to speak'; a profoundly deaf child is physically capable of speech but cannot learn to speak in the normal way, which is by imitating what he hears said. This may seem like common-sense, but the link between hearing and speech needs explanation as few, if any, people realise it intuitively. Also, 'speech' means 'language' as well as articulation; learning how to use words is equally dependent on imitation, which is why the reaction 'Well, at least they can read and write' shows a lack of understanding of the situation.

Nor does 'dumb' mean 'stupid'; a child may be multi-handicapped, both deaf and mentally handicapped, but deafness *per se* is not an intellectual handicap. From this, it is apparent that the results of deafness in infancy and early childhood are totally different from those of deafness acquired in adulthood, and the two groups have little in common.

2. *Lip-reading.* It is only in popular fiction that it is possible to lip-read a bearded stranger side-view across a smoke-filled café! Lip-reading is in fact *very difficult*, even in ideal conditions, and relies largely on guesswork, as many sounds look alike on the lips; it is effective only in a one-to-one conversation.

3. *Hearing Aids.* These do *not* restore normal hearing in the same way that spectacles restore normal vision. Deafness is more often a problem of discrimination than lowered volume, so amplifying sound, which is what a hearing aid basically does, may be helpful but does not solve the problem.

4. *Sign Language.* This is *not* universal, but differs from country to country and is in fact far more regionally varied than spoken language because it has not been subjected to the standardising influence of the mass media. It is not merely a pantomimic representation of spoken language, but a language in its own right, with a grammatical structure which does not correspond to spoken English, for example.

The Christian Marriage Service Originally Included the Words 'Till **Death Us Do Part'**

The longer that you think about it, the stranger the phrase appears. In fact, it was not originally 'Till death us *do* part' or even 'Till death us *does* part' but 'Till death us *depart*' until 1662, when the verb 'depart' was still also transitive. It meant 'divide' or 'separate', and was used by Barrow in 1667, for example: "The closest union here cannot last longer than till death us depart".

It was in 1662 that 'depart' was changed in the marriage service to 'do part', grammatically also in the subjunctive mood and hence equally correct.

The American '**Declaration of Independence'** was Signed and Proclaimed on 4 July 1776

Montagu and Darling carefully demolish these fallacies (for there are three of them) in their *Ignorance of Certainty* (New York, 1970).

"It is a fact that members of the Second Continental Congress did *not* sign the document known to fame as the Declaration of Independence on 4 July 1776. American independence was *not* proclaimed to the world—as so often asserted—on that date. The official name of the document was *not* "the Declaration of Independence".

Firstly, independence was resolved—and the signing took place—on 2 July 1776. Secondly, it was on 3 July when the document was first published in two Pennsylvanian papers, the *Gazette* and the *Journal*. Congress voted on the Declaration on 4 July, but it was not until 8 July that the document was proclaimed by being read publicly from the balcony of Independence Hall. Thirdly, the official title of the document is "The Unanimous Declaration of the Thirteen United States of America", the word 'Independence' occurring nowhere in the title.

Dental Fallacies

"Clean teeth never decay" is a fallacy promulgated by at least one manufacturer of toothpaste. A clean surface is desirable, but impossible to obtain, owing to the perennial omnipresence of bacteria. However, the truism that toothpaste, dental floss, and brushing must all fail in various ways to prevent decay (they can only at best reduce the *speed* of decay) should not be taken by any youngster as an excuse to avoid brushing the teeth to remove as much as possible of accretions caused by eating and drinking. One's *general* health is a factor as important as frequent brushing in dental health.

It is frequently believed that 'primitive' peoples

suffer less from tooth decay than do more 'civilized' peoples. This ignores the sugar-chewing Jamaicans, whose teeth decayed long before the white man arrived, and the Neanderthaloid 'Rhodesian' man of about 30,000 years ago was found to have decay in nearly every tooth of the upper jaw. The generalization is, however, true in the case of metropolitan white men vis-à-vis Zulus: according to V. Suk *(American Journal of Physical Anthropology,* vol. 2, 1919, pp. 351–88), at the age of 18, only 10–15 percent of the former have, 'perfect' teeth, while the figure among the latter is 85–94 percent.

An interesting fallacy, recurring in 1976 *(The Penguin medical encyclopedia,* 2nd ed., p. 433), is the old notion that "human jaws have receded in the course of evolution, and there is now barely room for the full set of permanent teeth". But there never was. Adolph H. Schutz, writing in *Current Anthropology* (vol. 7, 1966, p. 356), states that "unequivocal crowding of teeth is quite common among recent wild monkeys and apes. I have never failed to encounter cases with displaced, twisted, or impacted single or several large teeth in collections of primate skulls, and often such manifestations of unmistakable maladjustment in the size of the teeth and the jaws, resulting in crowding, are much more pronounced than in the two or three instances found in the Australopithecines".

Human teeth constitute irrefragable evidence, according to some, that Man is essentially a meat-eater, with the natural ability to rend animal flesh. Nothing could be more absurd: comparative anatomy proves the frugivorous and *not* the carnivorous origin of Man.

Diamonds *Cannot be Split*
by a Hammer on an Anvil

Diamond is graded 15 on the 15-point Mohs Hardness Scale, and is thus the *hardest* substance known, but it is relatively *brittle*. Yet Pliny the Elder convinced antiquity (and the belief persisted until the 19th century in diamond-rich South Africa) that 'these stones are tested upon the anvil, and will resist the blow to such an extent as to make the iron rebound and the very anvil split asunder'. There are so many errors in Pliny that one is tempted to wonder whether he was writing, delightedly, with tongue in cheek to discover whether he could indeed fool all of the people all of the time.

In 1476, Swiss mercenaries found diamonds belonging to Charles the Bold, Duke of Burgundy, after the Battle of Morat, and struck them to test for genuineness. They powdered—so they were!

The clever French jeweller Jean-Baptiste Tavernier (1605–1689), who visited the Indian diamond mines in the 17th century, found that some merchants knew the true facts, but persuaded simple miners that their diamonds were not real by breaking them with a hammer. They proceeded to make away with the pieces after the disappointed miners had left.

*"What the **Dickens!**"*
Derives from Charles Dickens

The common expression has nothing to do with *any* member of the Dickens family at all, but is simply a euphemism (via 'Dickson') for "What the Devil!" coined in a more squeamish age than our own.

Diogenes of Sinope Lived in a Tub

No reference to this legend is made in the authoritative article by K. von Fritz in the 2nd ed. of the *Oxford classical dictionary* (1970). His main principles were that happiness is attained by satisfying only one's natural needs and by satisfying them in the cheapest and easiest way. What is natural cannot be dishonourable or indecent and therefore can and should be done in public. Conventions which are contrary to these principles are unnatural and should not be observed.

Diogenes' biographer, Seneca, wrote over three hundred years after the death of Diogenes that "a man so crabbed ought to have lived in a tub like a dog". E. Cobham Brewer, in *A dictionary of phrase and fable*, corrupts this to "Diogenes. A noted Greek cynic philosopher (about 412–323 B.C.), who, according to Seneca, lived in a tub . . ." A textbook example, perhaps, of the rise of a common fallacy.

Some People Are **Double-Jointed**

No: there are no recorded cases of this. People commonly said to be 'double-jointed' have ligaments holding the end of the two articulating bones slightly looser than customary, thus permitting greater freedom in the relative movements of their parts.

Dowsers *Have an Ability to Find Water Wherever It Exists*

Dowsing or water-divining is a practice which has been recorded from a period almost as early as that when we first encounter astrology. Despite the impossibility of the forked twig in the diviner's hands responding to the non-existent 'magnetism' of water, it is true that dowsers have succeeded in locating water after trained geologists have failed to locate any. But the majority of dowsers do *not* possess any exceptional gift: they find water where the beginner would also find it. What assists them is the subconscious registration and interpretation of certain phenomena and their emergence into consciousness by means of a psychological automatism, normally twitching. The dowser has previously discovered water in terrain similar to that where he now suddenly twitches: indications include slight changes in the colour and type of vegetation or soil, visible and tactile evidence of the ground underfoot, even the smell of a wettish area, or the slight sound made by an underground stream near the surface which would be undetected by the layman. Dowsers are notoriously more successful in areas where water has already been found in abundance, and less so where water is known to be scarce, indicating a connection with luck.

Dragonflies *Sting*

The dragonfly *(Libellula)* belongs to the order *Neuroptera:* none of the *Neuroptera* stings. The dragonfly lives on flies and other insects captured on the wing, and if you are lucky enough to entice a wandering dragonfly into a room infested with mosquitoes, you will soon have an insect-free environment and a well-contented dragonfly.

A Little Dutch Boy Put His Finger in a **Dyke** to Save the City of Haarlem

The Dutch have ridiculed since 1873, when the story was apparently first invented by an American, the legend that a brave urchin sacrificed his life to save his native Haarlem from being flooded. He is alleged to have kept his finger in the hole in the dyke wall, though it did not occur to the readers that the amount of water that might trickle through a hole small enough to be stuffed by a little boy's finger might not in fact be quite so lethal, after all. Better, perhaps, if he had simply run to warn the inhabitants of Haarlem.

But the picturesque will usually drive out common sense when the two are in conflict, and the Netherlands Tourist Association has bowed to the weight of error by erecting a bronze statue to the invented lad.

E

Earwigs are So Called
Because They Hide in Human and Animal Ears

It seems that they were so called (in most languages, not only in English: cf. *auricularia, gusano del oido, perce-oreille, Ohrwurm,* etc.) because the rear wings suggest the shape of a human ear, and that this name then induced the folk-belief that they hid in human ears. That they do not in fact do so seems commonly accepted by entomologists. One reason is that the human ear contains bitter wax as a repellent against such invasions, and another is that earwigs eat vegetable matter and would have no interest in the perils of inhabiting human or animal ears.

Brown *Eggs* are More Nutritious Than White

Not so. British mothers are taught so by their grandmothers and so do not question the belief. Similarly, American mothers are told by their grandmothers that white eggs are purer than brown. The colour is simply laid on by the bird for its own purposes long after the contents of the shell, and even the shell itself, are completed. The chemical composition in all eggs of the same species of bird appears to be the same.

Egyptological and Pyramidological Theories

Top Stone Books offer a 96-page book by E. R. Capt, *The Great Pyramid decoded,* on what they call 'the most mysterious building in the world'. But there is nothing whatsoever mysterious about the Pyramid of Cheops, known by reason of its size as the Great Pyramid or about any of the other eighty or so Pyramids scattered about the Nile Valley.

For a hundred years it has been known by excavation and by hieroglyphic inscriptions to have been the tomb of the Pharaoh Khufu *(Gk.* Cheops), but the successful decipherment of hieroglyphics and sophisticated archaeological techniques have not prevented Peter Kolosimo and many hundreds of others from foisting their opinions to the contrary on the gullible public. Kolosimo claims some mystic significance for his hypotheses that "the distance of the Cheops Pyramid from the centre of the world is the same as its distance from the North Pole", that "the Great Pyramid meridian passes through more land than any other meridian", and that "the height of the Great Pyramid is in direct relationship with the distance of our planet from the sun" (see Kolosimo's *Not of this world*, London, 1970, p. 240). As for the first point, the same is true—surely it goes without saying—for all other monuments on the same latitude; as for the second point, more land seems to pass through other meridians (though it seems a matter of dubious significance); and as for the third, the reader will point out as gently as he sees fit that the height of the Great Pyramid is in 'direct relationship' with the height of most other things, in the same way that the number 64 is in 'direct relationship' with the numbers 1, 2, 4, 8, 16, and 32, not to mention 128 and 256.

Another pyramidological curiosity is G. R. Riffert's *The Great Pyramid* (5th ed., London, 1935), which claims to the author's satisfaction, if to nobody else's, that the existence of the Great Pyramid is a proof of the existence of God. [But surely therefore a god of the *Egyptian* pantheon, rather than a Judeo-Hellenistic one?]

Winifred Needler has contributed to the world's store of common sense on pyramidology in *Popular Archaeology* (October 1972) by observing that "a formula constructed with sufficient complexity may fit a given phenomenon and yet prove nothing". This statement was made *à propos* of Peter Tompkins' book *Secrets of the Great Pyramid* (London, 1971), yet another of the yearly crop of theories which 'explain' aspects of the Pyramids as if orthodox archaeology had some mad reason for suppressing the true nature of Egyptian funerary architecture in its historical development.

Elephants are Afraid of Mice

Cartoonists and others have often shown an elephant cowering away from a mouse. Those who work in elephants' stalls either in zoos or in circuses have from time to time seen mice running about not far from the elephant but, far from panicking, it seems that the elephants—mainly due to their relatively poor vision—cannot even see the mice.

Elephants Live to an Age of 100 Years or More

It has been reported at second hand, even by some biologists, that elephants are frequently longer-lived than men, though the longest-lived human being reliably known is the 113-year-old Delina Filkins (New York), born in 1815 and deceased in 1928.

By contrast, the oldest known elephant, Kyaw Thee (Burma) died at 70 in 1965, though Modoc (died in 1975 at Irvine, California) *may* have been as old as the 78 years claimed at death.

Foreign **Embassies** are 'On Foreign Soil'

It is popular wisdom that embassies and consulates are, in effect, part of their own national territory. British police, for example, never enter an embassy in London without the ambassador's prior permission. Similarly, Russian police have tried to prevent would-be defectors from entering the British Embassy in Moscow, but have never crossed the threshold in pursuit. The Vienna Convention of 1961, which set the present code of practice on diplomatic immunity, says that diplomatic premises are inviolable, and the host state has a 'special duty' to protect them. But the ruling is unclear on people held against their will, or seeking political asylum in an embassy, as in the famous case of Cardinal Mindszenty, who lived for years in the American Embassy in Budapest.

But foreign embassies in Britain are on English soil, not foreign, according to a ruling of Mr. Justice Cumming–Bruce in the High Court on 11 May 1972. The matter arose in a case involving the attempt to validate a Talak divorce obtained by a husband in a ceremony at the United Arab Republic (now the Arab Republic of Egypt) Consulate. Mr Justice Cumming–Bruce ruled against the Egyptian-born Mr Jan Pierre Radwan, who had claimed that his Talak divorce (in which he said of his wife "I divorce thee" thrice) was valid in English law.

Mr Justice Cumming-Bruce was "satisfied that the

53

term 'extra territoriality' has been used to describe, in a compendium phrase, that bundle of immunities and privileges which are accorded by receiving States to envoys sent by foreign States.

The building occupied by a foreign embassy and the land upon which it stands are part of the territory of the receiving State and are therefore under the jurisdiction of the receiving State though members occupying it are primarily under the jurisdiction of the Sending State".

'Epicureanism' is Synonymous with Gluttony

The word 'epicure' has come to be applied to anyone devoted to the pleasures of the table. Epicurus (341–270 B.C.) on the contrary held that philosophy consisted in the wise conduct of life, to be attained by reliance on the evidence of the senses, and by the elimination of superstition and of the belief in supernatural intervention. His ethics teach that pleasure is the only good, but by this he intimated that a perfect harmony of body and mind is to be sought in plain living, and in virtue.

F

Fairy Rings

Fairy rings are caused by a circular-seeding fungus which, by its annual decay, renders the soil unfit for a new crop of fungus but increases the fertility of the ground. There consequently appears a gradually increasing circle of grass which is greener than the surrounding turf. The traditional explanation, harmless enough to those who don't mind misleading ignorant children into a lifetime of superstition by the primrose path of faery, is that such rings spring up where fairies habitually dance, or grow above a subterranean fairy village. E. and M. A. Radford's *Encyclopedia of superstitions* (London, 1961) observes that if anyone ran nine times round such a ring on the night of the full moon, he would hear the fairies laughing and talking below. Walter P. Wright, in *An illustrated encyclopedia of gardening* (London, 1932) advocates not running round the ring but destroying it "by syringing with a pound of sulphate of iron dissolved in three gallons of water". It is not recorded what the fairies thought of Walter Wright.

'Fall' is the American Word for 'Autumn'

There is nothing American about the use of 'Fall' for the third season of the year other than its current use in the United States; both 'Fall' and 'Autumn' have a long European ancestry: the latter from the Latin 'autumnus' (possibly from Etruscan?), and the former from the Old English 'feallan', akin to the Old Frisian 'falla'.

'Fall' in this sense can be found in the works of

Raleigh, Drayton, and other writers of the Elizabethan period.

The **Faust** Story in European Literature is Based on Legend

An absurd concoction of implausible tales on a figure called Johann Faust was published under the title of *Historia von D. Joh. Fausten* (Frankfurt, 1575) by the printer Johann Spiess. The sensational booklet, containing a direful warning against theological heresies, among them necromancy, was reprinted, translated, and rewritten for popular consumption all over Europe in succeeding centuries, until Christopher Marlowe created the *Tragicall history of Dr Faustus* in 1588–1589 (entered in the Stationers' Register in 1604 but apparently not published in 1604).

From England the tragedy returned to Germany, where Gotthold Ephraim Lessing made the heretic into an altruistic lover of knowledge who deserved salvation in fragments of a play, *Faust* (1759). It was left to the great Goethe to produce the most lasting works on the story of Faust (complete edition, 1834), which completely transform the medieval story. Faust is saved in Goethe's epic drama. Other treatments of the story include the operas *Faust* by Gounod and *Mefistofele* by Boïto, Paul Valéry's *Mon Faust*, and Thomas Mann's *Doctor Faustus*.

Johann Faust was, however, a real man—a travelling magician and mountebank who lived in Germany from the 1480s to about 1540. He is mentioned by Trithemius (b. 1462) in a letter dated 1507, and by several other contemporaries, including the demonologist

Wierus, who states that Faustus was a drunkard who had studied magic at Cracow and was eventually strangled by Satan after his house had been shaken by a tremendous din.

Fish are Especially Good for the Brain

This fallacy, propagated in dozens of Bertie Wooster stories and novels by P. G. Wodehouse (on whom otherwise be blessing), appears ultimately to derive from the views of the German philosopher Friedrich Büchner (1824–1899), that "without phosphorus there is no thought"; of the French chemist Jean Dumas (1800–1884) that "fish are a rich source of phosphorus"; and finally of the Swiss naturalist Jean Louis Agassiz (1807–1873) that "fish are good for the brain".

This assumption ignores the fact that phosphorus occurs in many foods other than fish, and the further fact that other foods are equally good for the brain.

"There is no foundation whatever for this view", stated Sir Henry Thompson in *Food and feeding*, and Dr Charles Hill ('The Radio Doctor') declared that "as for brain food, there are no foods for the brain except work".

Fish Can Fly

Not one of the hundred or so species of 'flying fish' can actually fly in the commonly accepted sense. They do, however, have enlarged pectoral fins which enable them to glide just above the sea's surface at a maximum of ten miles an hour for a maximum of two hundred yards. They usually glide to escape predators such as dolphins.

Food *From a Dented or Opened Can Should Not be Eaten*

Food in damaged cans will only be contaminated if germs have entered through a split in the tin. Otherwise, food from opened tins is no more susceptible to infection than is fresh food. The cans themselves cannot cause poisoning.

Fox-Hunting *Has Been Popular in Britain Since Medieval Times*

Not at all. British fox-hunting as a popular field sport dates from the latter part of the 18th century. The first reference to hunting the fox occurs as early as 1278, but the most popular field sports in Britain until medieval times were hunting the boar, the deer, and the hare.

'Frankenstein' *Was a Monster*

By analogy, possibly, with Bram Stoker's fictional Count Dracula, Mary Wollstonecraft Shelley's *Frankenstein* (1818) is often believed to be a story of an eponymous monster, but Frankenstein was an imaginary student of medicine in Geneva who learnt the secret of imparting life to inanimate matter and, after constructing the semblance of a human being from bones gathered in charnel-houses, gives it life. The creature inspires all who view it with fear and loathing, and it comes to feel only hatred for its creator. It kills Frankenstein's brother, his bride, Frankenstein and finally itself.

Freckles Can Be Removed by Lemon Juice

"*Nothing* will remove freckles", write Ashley Montagu and Edward Darling in *The prevalence of nonsense* (New York, 1967). "At least, nothing will remove freckles *only*. There are preparations which will remove the skin, if that's what you want. Then the freckles disappear".

Freckles are a series of small areas of pigmentation usually evoked by exposure to the chemically active ultraviolet rays of the sun, but since most of these pigment cells do not reach the dead surface layer forming the outermost portion of the skin, no substance applied to the surface of the skin can have any effect on those cells which lie deeper.

Preparations sold to remove freckles are, so far, all believed fraudulent and can cause injury to the skin.

Warm Water **Freezes** *Sooner Than Cold*

A fallacy which even caught out the illustrious Francis Bacon (*Novum organum*, 1620). The reverse is the case.

There is an interesting exception which is not

widely appreciated. Water which has been boiled and then cooled to the same temperature as the cold fresh water will freeze just ahead of the other, probably because the boiling process drives off the carbonic acid gas and air, and deposits any calcium carbonate previously in solution.

I suppose that, as boys, many of us remember pouring boiling water on a snowy hillside to make a slide, but the true purpose of that is to make for a smooth surface once the snow has frozen again.

Frogs Fall from the Sky

Robert Plot's important, ambitious *The natural history of Staffordshire* (Oxford, 1686) is one of the many books in dozens of languages responsible for this fallacy. In Michael Paffard's view, the man responsible for hoaxing Plot was Walter Chetwynd of Ingestre Hall, who also offered his guest, then Keeper of the Ashmolean Museum, 'potted otter' which Plot found to be "indistinguishable from venison, which it probably was". Chetwynd described to the credulous but enthusiastic Plot how frogs had showered down from the sky and were afterwards found in very great numbers even upon the leads of the stately gatehouse at Ingestre. Plot concludes that sometimes "the Spawn or Seed of Frogs may be either blowne from the tops of Mountains, or drawn up with the Vapours out of uliginous places, and be brought to perfection in the Clouds, and discharged thence in Showers", though he prefers to think frogs more often "produced on the surface of the Earth . . . by a Fermentation excited in the Dust".

This of course provoked other fantastic tales of

frogs, such as the live frog allegedly encased in the solid stone of the pinnacle of Statfold church steeple. He did not find it incredible that a creature "of so slender a dyet" should remain in such a situation "without meat or air" for some hundreds of years.

It rains frogs, of course, because after rainfall frogs suddenly emerge. But conversely, frogs never emerge in dry weather if they can avoid it because they can only survive if their skin is moist, so they are bound to live near damp places, such as rainbarrels or stagnant ponds. So, when it appears to 'rain frogs', in fact the frogs (or ageing tadpoles) were there all the time, but unperceived.

Charles Fort, in his amusing *The book of the damned* (New York, 1919) records the 'raining' not only of frogs, calves, and milk, but also mentions popular press accounts of raining fish, fungi, stones (some of them inscribed), protoplasm, hatchets, masks, and ceremonial regalia. Most of the fish fall on India, if one judges by the preponderance of newspaper reports.

G

Galileo Defied the Inquisition with the Words *"Eppur Si Muove" (Yet It* Does *Move)*

The publication of Galileo Galilei's *Dialogo dei due massimi sistemi del mondo* (Florence, 1632) evoked enormous interest, and provoked ecclesiastical animosity for its defence of the Copernican theory of a heliocentric solar system, as opposed to the orthodox geocentric view. In August the book was banned and in October Galileo was summoned by the Papal Inquisition to Rome. He was finally examined on 21 June 1633, and on the following day recanted.

'Everybody knows' that he rose from his feet after recanting, stamped his foot in anger, and shouted defiantly "Eppur si muove"—"Yet [the Earth] *does* move". The error persists in 1978 (assertion by Renée Haynes —"Eppur se muove" [sic] wrote Galileo—in *The Times Literary Supplement,* 17 March 1978) and in 1979, on p. 89 of *Famous last words* (London, 1979) compiled by Jonathon Green.

In fact, the first record we have of this 'saying' appears as late as 1761, one hundred and nineteen years after the death of Galileo. The source is the notoriously unreliable *Querelles littéraires* (vol. 3, p. 49) by the Abbé Irailli. See Giorgio di Santillana, *The crime of Galileo* (London, 1958).

Roman *'Gaul'* Was Modern France

It was in fact much more extensive, including the Low Countries, Switzerland, and parts of northern Italy, in addition to continental France. Allcroft and Plaistowe, in their edition of Caesar's *Gallic War,* Book I, write:

"In the time of Caesar the Gauls occupied roughly the whole of that part of Europe which lies west of the Rhine and north of the Pyrenees, together with much of Switzerland, and that part of the Italian peninsula which lies to the north of the rivers Rubicon and Macra (thence called Gallia Cisalpina). They had once overrun the land as far as the Tiber, and had routed the Etruscans and settled in the Po Valley; but in the year 218 B.C. the Romans had planted the colonies of Placentia and Cremona as the symbol and safeguard of the final reduction or expulsion of these Cisalpine Gauls."

All **Gaul** is Divided Into Three Parts

Possibly the most famous sentence in Latin literature is that which opens *De bello Gallico* by Julius Caesar: "Gallia est omnis divisa in partes tres, quarum unam incolunt Belgae, aliam Aquitani, tertiam, qui ipsorum lingua Celtae, nostra Galli appellantur" (All Gaul is divided into three parts, one inhabited by the Belgae, another by the Aquitani, and the third by the people whom we call Galli, and who call themselves Celtae).

But Caesar is of course wrong, and he knows he is. He has deliberately omitted Gallia Narbonensis, also called Gallia Braccata *(braccae* = breeches) from the custom of wearing the national breeches. Gallia Narbonensis was named after Narbo (modern Narbonne) and covered much of modern Provence.

Caesar's subject was Gallia Comata, the land of the tribespeople whom he wished to tame by force of arms.

"The real puzzle is not the best translation of *omnis*, but why the Belgae and the Aquitani should apparently be denied the name Celt. In the case of the Aquitani the answer is simple: with the exception of one tribe, the Bituriges Vivisci, at the mouth of the Garonne, they were 'different in physique and language from the Celtae and more like the Iberians' (Strabo 4,176 and 189,2); and in fact it is tempting to call them Iberians outright, because their race would then bestride the Pyrenees as the Basques do today", according to D. B. Gregor (*Celtic*, Cambridge, 1980).

The **Giraffe** Has More Cervical Vertebrae Than Any Other Mammal

Because of its long neck, the giraffe is the subject of this observation by most visitors to zoos or wildlife parks. So just check on your next visit to a science museum: like man, the whale, and all other mammals, the giraffe has seven cervical vertebrae.

Venetian **Glass** is Made in Venice

The particular sand needed for Venetian glass is not found in Venice, but in Murano—an island in the lagoon easily accessible by regular *vaporetto*—and that is where 'Venetian' glass has always been made. The glassblowers are still active on Murano, and a visit to them, with the fine early church on neighbouring Torcello, is an integral part of any holiday in the Veneto.

The **Great Dane** Is a Breed of Danish Dogs

The Great Dane, the largest breed within the European mastiff family, is not connected with Denmark in any way so far historically recorded.

In the 16th century, Great Danes were most frequently known as 'English Dogges', and about 1680 they were bred in great numbers at the princely courts in Germany. The largest and best of the breed were called 'Chamber Dogs' *(Kammerhunde)* and wore gilded collars, while the lesser animals were known as 'Life Dogs' *(Leibhunde)* and wore collars with a silver finish. At the first German dog show, held at Hamburg in 1863, "some very grave-looking Doggen took part in the event". Of these, 8 were said to be 'Danish Doggen' and 7 announced as 'Ulmer Doggen'. "The truth is", confides *The new complete Great Dane* (New York, 1974), "that of all these dogs not one had ever seen Denmark, nor had any of them even been born there, as their papers indicated." At the 1876 show, the judges called the Great Dane the 'Deutsche Dogge', as it had been called for centuries.

The Word **'Gremlin'** was Invented During World War II

On the radio programme *Desert island discs* (British Broadcasting Corporation, 27 October 1979), the writer Roald Dahl claimed to have invented the word 'gremlin' during the Second World War.

B. J. Watson of Hull, in a letter to *Radio Times* (1–7 December 1979), claimed however that the word was already familiar to readers of *The Aeroplane*, where it occurs three times in a poem published on 10 April 1929. Gremlins are "mischievous imps which inhabited aircraft and were held responsible for all the unaccountable failures, both mechanical and human, which occurred. They were particularly active during the War when there were, of course, many more unexplainable incidents".

The earliest published evidence for 'gremlin' in the 1972 Supplement to *The Oxford English Dictionary* is dated 1941, but Dr R. E. Allen, Senior Editor of the Oxford dictionaries, writes: "The only additional information we have in our files is an unverified reference to *Newsweek* of 7 September 42, which is said to trace the word back to 1923" [personal communication, 1979].

The **Gryphon**

Lewis Carroll, who wrote a great deal on logic and mathematics, peopled Alice's Wonderland with both real and imaginary animals, so that children who know Bill the Lizard and the White Rabbit find no difficulty in accepting the objective reality of the gryphon. After all, one might argue, if the luckless dodo once existed, might not the gryphon have done so too?

Certainly the Greeks believed the fabulous beasts to inhabit Scythia, where they guarded Scythian gold. But by the 17th century, the belief was falling gradually into desuetude. As Sir Thomas Browne writes: "That there are Griffons in Nature, that is a mixt and dubious animall, in the fore-part resembling an Eagle, and behinde the shape of Lion, with erected eares, foure feet, and a long taile, many affirme, and most I perceive deny not; the same is averred by Aelian, Solinus, Mela, and Herodotus, countenanced by the name sometimes found in Scripture, and was an Hieroglyphick of the Egyptians.

"Notwithstanding wee finde most diligent enquirers to be of a contrary assertion; for beside that Albertus and Pliny have disallowed it, the learned Aldrovand hath in a large discourse rejected it; Mathias Michovius who write of those Northerne parts wherein men place these Griffins, hath positively concluded against it, and if examined by the doctrine of animals, the invention is monstrous, nor much inferiour unto the figment of Sphynx, Chimaera, and Harpies: for though some species there be of a middle and participating natures, that is, of bird and beast, as we finde the Bat to be, yet are their parts so conformed and set together that we cannot define the beginning or end of either, there being a commixtion of both in the whole, rather then an adaptation, or cement of the one unto the other".

Gryphons don't exist.

Dr Guillotin Invented the **Guillotine**

An understandable mistake, but he merely encouraged the machine's use in the interest of a painless death. It was invented by a German mechanic called Schmidt under the direction of Dr Antonin Louise, and was thus known first as a 'Louison' or 'Louisette'.

Neither was Guillotin the first victim of the machine—that was the highwayman Pelletier (25 April 1792). Guillotin outlived the Revolution by twenty years, dying at the age of 76 on 26 May 1814.

H

Cutting or Shaving *Hair*
Affects Its Speed of Growth

Cutting hair has no effect at all on its growth. Shaving is believed to thicken hair because newly-shaved stubble feels rough.

Hair Can Turn White Naturally Overnight

Normally through fear, horror, or terror, goes the well-authenticated story in the cases reported by *Time:* 2 March 1942 (C. Yates McDaniel, after witnessing 'the collapse of Singapore at close hand'); 31 May 1943 (Ernie Pyle, whose hair merely turned grey during the African campaign); 14 August 1944 (Air Marshal Coningham); and 4 September 1944 (Jimmie Hines, but over a period of three years, in Sing Sing).

However, this is ridiculous in the light of due natural processes, and all recorded cases of 'overnight' bleaching are either exaggerated, or due to bleaching or the sudden removal of artificial colour. In their *Diseases of the skin*, R. L. Sutton and R. L. Sutton, Jr. write, "Sudden, overnight blanching, reliably reported, is doubtless the result of the removal of cosmetic coloration or the application of a bleach. Physiological and anatomical facts are incompatible with the possibility of actual, nonartificial, instant blanching".

Hair on Men's Bodies Is a Sign of Strength

This curious fallacy probably derives from the Biblical story of Samson and his hair. Ordinary daily observation by doctors shows no correlation whatsoever between the amount of hair on a man's body and his actual or potential strength.

A man with hair on his chest is commonly thought to be uncommonly strong, 'like a gorilla'. The gorilla has hair on his belly, his back, his shoulders, arms and legs, but none on his chest.

Richard *Hakluyt* Was a Great Traveller and Founded the Hakluyt Society

The greatest anthology of writings on the voyages and discoveries of the Elizabethans is Richard Hakluyt's *The principal navigations, voiages, traffiques and discoveries of the English nation* (3 vols., London, 1598–1600). It contains over 1,700,000 words, and includes all the English-language writings he could find, as well as translations from several European languages. The one-volume edition of 1589 was superseded by the definitive 3-volume edition which was to be described by James Anthony Froude as 'the prose epic of the modern English nation'. However, Hakluyt himself—though he corresponded with Mercator and Ortelius, and met Drake, Frobisher, Gilbert and Raleigh—never travelled farther than France. The Hakluyt Society named in his honour and still flourishing today was founded as late as 1846.

As *Heavy as Lead*

It is frequently believed, following the saying that
something is 'as heavy as lead', that lead must be the
heaviest element. In fact, 'heavy' is the wrong adjective to use in this context: the correct word is 'dense'.
The densest element known, since its discovery in
1804, is in fact osmium (22–59 grams per cubic centi-
metre), so one should more accurately be saying 'as
dense as osmium'.

Platinum, uranium and tungsten are also all
'heavier than lead'!

Helen of Troy was Abducted by Paris

'Everyone knows' that Helen, wife of Menelaus, was
abducted by Paris. Andromache curses Helen with the
words: "The beauty of your glance has brought / This
rich and noble country to a shameful end".

In Euripides' *Trojan women* (lines 368 ff.), Cassan-
dra states that the war was caused by the folly [a euphemism for the imperialistic zeal] of the Greeks, and
Helen herself freely admits (1.946) that she eloped
with Paris of her own accord.

Vellacott sums up the situation thus: "Euripides
shows how the precise interest of an intellectual theory, and the helpless anguish of a human being, both
contribute to that Greek propensity for fixing the
blame on some convenient scapegoat, which demonstrated itself in innumerable cruelties throughout
Greek history and, as Thucydides observed, reached a
new level of atrocity in the Peloponnesian War".

A Galloping **Horse** Always Has
at Least One Hoof on the Ground

It is astounding that the fallacy should have survived the demonstration of about 1878 by the photographer Eadweard Muybridge (1830–1904, an Englishman who emigrated to the U.S.A. in 1852) which actually culminated in a book, called *Animal locomotion* (11 vols., Philadelphia, 1887). Every so often the newspapers publish photographs which again demonstrate this well-known fact. The difficulty is that the tiny fraction of a second when all four feet are off the ground cannot be detected by the human eye unaided.

Drinking **Hot Tea** Cools the Body

A very widespread fallacy, which was exploded by Dr Leonard Williams, in the London *Evening Standard* of 25 May 1922, among others. It derives from the relative coolness we feel shortly after *raising* the temperature by drinking hot tea. The drinking of hot tea during a heat wave might in fact cause heat stroke if one were already very near to heat stroke. Drink cold water (but not too much or too quickly) in a heat wave. Cold water absorbs heat as we drink it, as its temperature has to be raised in our system from say 60°F to 98.5°F, our blood temperature. Thus, the drinking of a half a pint of cold water at 60°F absorbs 24 British thermal units, a large amount of useful heat.

The **Hundred Years' War**
Lasted for a Hundred Years

It might seem obvious to call a war by the length of time from beginning to end, but the Hundred Years' War between England and France lasted from 1337, in the reign of Edward III (the first action being a naval battle off Sluys), until 1453, in the reign of Henry VI (the last action being the battle of Castillon). The cause of the 'war', which was really an interrupted sequence of shorter wars, was the claim by England to the crown of France. The result was that the English were expelled from the whole of France except Calais.

'Husband' *Originally Meant a Married Man*

When Sir John Paston wrote to his mother, in 1475, that "I purpose to leeffe alle heer, and come home to you and be your hosbonde and balyff", he was merely using the term 'husband' in its true sense of a man who managed a household, as its head. *Hus* is the Anglo-Saxon for 'house' and 'bondi' the Old Norse for 'freeholder' or 'yeoman'.

We retain the original sense of the word in the verb 'to husband' *(sc.* one's resources) and the abstract noun 'husbandry'. A husband need not be married at all.

I

Ice Is White or Transparent, Like Water

The colour of ice, like that of water, is blue, and the colour is deep and intense in proportion to the thickness of clear ice or water through which the light passes. There is a great deal of persistent error about the blue colour of water. A good many people insist that it is due to the reflected blue colour of the sky. It is easy to prove that this is not so since the clear water of seas and lakes is seen to be blue when the sky is completely overcast.

The Word **'Idiot'** Originally Meant 'Mentally Defective'

The Greek *idiótes* denotes a private person, as opposed to someone fulfilling a public office. But, in ancient Greece, it was considered indispensable for the individual to obtain experience of public life, as part of his education. Those unqualified to take part in public life, whether mentally incapable, or simply untaught, were known as 'idiots'.

English writers understood the word in its original sense right up until the 17th century. Jeremy Taylor (1613–1667), who was at Caius College, Cambridge, wrote for example: "It is clear, by Bellarmine's confession, that S. Austin *[sc.* Augustine] affirmed that the plain places of Scripture are sufficient to all laics, and all *idiots* or private persons" *(A dissuasive from Popery).*

It is Illegal to **Impersonate** a Living Member of the Royal Family on the British Stage

Oddly enough this idea persists years after the restrictions were lifted (1968). Queen Elizabeth the Queen Mother was legally impersonated by Amanda Reiss in Royce Ryton's *Crown matrimonial* which opened at London's Haymarket Theatre on 19 October 1972.

Indian Ink Comes From India

The *Oxford English Dictionary* defines 'India ink' or 'Indian ink' as "a black pigment made in China and Japan sold in sticks; understood to consist of lampblack made into a paste with a solution of gum and dried. More accurately called *China ink*".

It is not clear how the designation 'Indian' arose, but Pepys used it in his diary entry for 5 November 1665: "Mr Evelyn, who . . . showed me most excellent painting in little, in distemper, India incke, water colours".

The Pope of the Roman Catholic Church Claims to be **Infallible**

Roman Catholics weary of repeating that this has never been the case. The statement of infallibility was first made at the Vatican Council of 1870, but refers only to occasions when the Pope speaks *ex cathedra*, that is from the Chair of St. Peter (metaphorically, of course; the chair on which he sits is several centuries later). In fact, there has so far been no occasion when he has proclaimed *ex cathedra,* so there has been no case in which the claim has been reasserted since 1870. Another fallacy is that infallibility began to operate only in 1870: it was predated to St. Peter himself. Laymen who point to the corruption and wickedness of certain popes are guilty of another fallacy: the Pope does not claim to be *impeccable.*

Influenza Is a New Disease

The pandemic of 1918–1919 killed some twenty million, most of them as a result of pneumonia or other complications, and it was perhaps the scale of that pandemic that persuaded most people that the disease is a product of the 20th century. Influenza (Italian, 'influence') was given its present name in 1741, but had been known earlier under other names, such as *grippe.*

As early as 1797, in *Medical and vulgar errors refuted,* John Jones ridiculed the fallacy that "the influenze . . . is a very dangerous distemper, and a new one; never known in this country till a few years ago". "It is neither a new nor a dangerous distemper", snorted the good Dr Jones.

J

'Jack' Is Short for 'John'

'Jack' is on the contrary short for 'Jacobus' (Latin for 'James') through the Old French 'Jaques' (modern French 'Jacques'). It has curiously enough come to be the commonest pet form of 'John', though the correct pet form 'Johnny' has its periods of ascendancy over the wrong word.

Jericho's (Late Bronze Age) Walls Came Tumbling Down

It must be true: it's in the Bible. John Garstang, who excavated at Jericho in the 1930s, announced that he had found the city's Late Bronze Age walls, which he ascribed to the time of Joshua, following Biblical tradition. The inner wall was discovered "to have fallen together with the remains of buildings upon it". Furthermore, the city had been destroyed by fire, "precisely in the manner described in the Book of Joshua". Garstang asserted beyond all doubt that "the destruction . . . corresponds in all material particulars with the Biblical narrative".

And so all laymen were taught, and believed, until Kathleen Kenyon returned to Jericho (or *Ariha* as it is known locally) in the 1950s with more scientifically-controlled techniques and a more open mind. She found that the fortifications dated by Garstang to the time of Joshua were a thousand years earlier in date.

Jesus Was Born in 4 B.C.

Even if one disagrees with the contention of those, like G. A. Wells *(Did Jesus exist?)*, who believe that Jesus Christ never actually existed, it is almost impossible to agree with the commonly-held views that he was born exactly 1980 years before 1980 Anno Domini, or that he was born in 4 'Before Christ', a paradox that is nevertheless widely believed. Dean Inge, in *Outspoken essays* (London, 1921) asserted that "Jesus was born at Nazareth about four years before the Christian era", and this folklore represents the popular view in the 19th and early 20th centuries.

Stuart Campbell of Edinburgh has kindly provided the following comments: "The Christian dating system was established in the 6th century by a Greek monk, Dionysius Exiguus, who sensibly used Luke's claim that Jesus was 30 years old when he began to preach. If John had begun his preaching one year before Jesus, and that was Tiberius' 15th year (again according to Luke), then the terminal year is correct, Tiberius' 15th year being 29 C.E.

But those who believe in the historicity of the Massacre of the Innocents at Bethlehem, and believe that the Herod who ruled at the time of Jesus' birth was Herod the Great, must put back the date of birth at least to 4 B.C., when this Herod died. But Herod was a family name, and both the sons of Herod the Great, Antipas and Archaelus, also bore the name 'Herod'. Thus the Gospel's reference to 'Herod the King' is not sufficient evidence to justify the conclusion that the king in question was Herod the Great himself.

Furthermore, if one wishes to harmonise the date of Jesus' birth with the story of the census, then the event must be moved *forward* to 6 C.E., when

83

Sulpicius Quirinius conducted the assessment of Judaea, upon the assumption by Rome of direct rule over that province. The association of Jesus with this assessment was probably contrived by someone anxious to find a reason to move Jesus to Bethlehem for his birth (in fulfilment of prophecy). In fact the Roman assessment did not require such movement of population.

The date of birth given in *The Oxford Dictionary of the Christian Church* (London, 1957, p. 723) is 'not more than three or four years before' the death of King Herod the Great (4 B.C.). The *Catholic Biblical Encyclopedia* (New York, 1949, p. 76) comes down in favour of 8 B.C.

The Maid of Orleans Was Called *Joan of Arc* or *Jeanne D'Arc*

She is now, but it is a fallacy to think that she came from a village called Arc, because there simply isn't one near her home town of Domrémy. Littré confirms that the name was spelt Darc on all contemporary documents, and that she was the daughter of a farmer, Jacques Darc. She was not canonized until 1920.

Joseph Wore a Coat of Many Colours

Much more picturesque than the truth, but the *Cambridge Bible* editors kindly divest us of yet another appalling mistranslation. Joseph, according to the orig-

84

inal Hebrew, wore 'a long garment with sleeves'. But as there is no reliable support for the tales of Joseph, regrettably even that emendation seems to do little service.

K

Helen **Keller** was Born Blind, Deaf, and Dumb

There is a widespread belief that the blind deaf mute Helen Adams Keller (1880–1968) was born with all her disabilities, but in fact she was born entirely normal.

It was in 1881 that the infant was struck by what may have been scarlet fever, from which she recovered with so many faculties tragically impaired. The gradual acquisition of her independence, with the loving aid of Anne Sullivan Macy, Polly Thompson, and Winifred Corbally, is one of the most inspiring examples of the power of the human spirit to transcend physical handicaps. Mark Twain remarked: "The two most interesting people of the last one hundred years are Helen Keller and the Emperor Napoleon Bonaparte".

Krakatoa Is East of Java

The volcanic island forming the subject of the film *Krakatoa, East of Java,* directed by Bernard L. Kowalski in the late 1960s, is not of course east of Java at all.

A glance at the map of Indonesia shows that the island (properly spelt Rakata) lies at latitude 6° 11′ S. and longitude 105° 26′ E., that is of course *west* of Java. The film is melodramatic and over-romanticised, glossing over the real horror when more than fortythousand people lost their lives in the eruptions of 1883.

L

Winston Churchill was Present
At the First Relief of **Ladysmith**

As a correspondent of the *Morning Post*, the young Winston Churchill described the first relief of Ladysmith as an eyewitness, but Thomas Pakenham, in *The Boer War* (London, 1979) proves that Churchill was miles away from Ladysmith at the time.

Jesus and the Disciples Sat Down
at the **Last Supper**

Probably the most famous depiction in art of the story told in Mark, Matthew and Luke of the Lord's Supper, also known as the Last Supper, is the wall-painting in oil tempera by Leonardo da Vinci still to be seen adjoining the damaged Church of Santa Maria delle Grazie in Milan. It was painted in 1495–1498, and shows Jesus and his disciples seated around a table.

Sir Thomas Browne, in *Pseudodoxia Epidemica* (London, 1646), put the record straight, even if he went unheeded. "Concerning the pictures of the Jews, and Easterne Nations at their feasts, concerning the gesture of our Saviour at the Passeover, who is usually described sitting upon a stoole or bench at a square table, in the middest of the twelve, many make great doubt; and though they concede a table jesture will hardly allow this usuall way of Session. Wherein restrayning no mans enquiry, it will appeare that accubation, or lying downe at meales was a gesture used by very many nations. That the Parthians used it, is evident from Athenaeus, who delivereth out of Possidonius, that their King lay downe at meales, on an

higher bed then others. That Cleopatra thus enter-
tained Anthonie, the same Author manifesteth when
he saith, shee prepared twelve Tricliniums".

Not only was the triclinium in almost ubiquitous
use around the Mediterranean at the time of Jesus
Christ, but we can actually see what the Last Supper
may have looked like, with the use of triclinia, in a
mosaic datable to 520 to 526 still to be seen at Sant'
Apollinare Nuovo, Ravenna.

Lead Pencils Contain Lead

The 'lead' in pencils is a compound of graphite and
clay or occasionally plumbago. The name was given to
it in the 16th-century when the contents were commonly believed to be lead, but were not even then.

Lemmings Commit Suicide

The lemming, a small rodent inhabiting the central
mountain chain of Norway and Sweden, is popularly
believed (if one can call the *Encyclopedia Britannica*,
14th ed., vol. 13, p. 905, a source and distillation of
popular belief) to 'descend . . . in countless multi-
tudes and proceed in a straight line until they reach
the sea, into which they plunge and are drowned'. The
reason for this lunacy is stated to be that their march
'is a survival from the old times when there was dry
land over the Baltic and North Seas'.

But lemmings have more sense than those who
write on their communal suicide for of course it has
never happened. They do breed in larger numbers in

certain years, and then if the food supply in the mountains is low, they do descend in varying numbers. They can and do swim streams, and it is probable that some reach the ocean and imagine that it is another small stream, get out of their depth, and drown. But the cosmic death wish is a fallacy, as is the regularity with which they are said to emerge from the mountains, as is their multiplicity. Most lemmings stay in the mountains. Not one has been known to commit suicide. John Masefield (in *The Lemmings*) declared that the fatal urge comes on them once in a hundred years, whereas Breland, in *Animal facts and fallacies* (London, 1950, pp. 62–3), claims that their feeding grounds become overpopulated roughly every three or four years.

One Cannot **Lie** and Tell the Truth Simultaneously

The lie or falsehood is a particular sensitive area of fallacy-theory, by which I refer to the importance of paradox in such statements as the demonstration that a man may lie and tell the truth at the same time by asserting that he is lying (in the 3rd-century *Lives of eminent philosophers* by Diogenes Laertius, translated by R. D. Hicks for the Loeb Classical Library, London, 1925).

If the reader still thinks that an argument *cannot* be valid if the conclusion contradicts a premise, ponder this example from Charles Hamblin's *Fallacies* (London, 1970):

> Epimenides was telling the truth when he said 'I am lying'.
> Therefore, Epimenides was lying when he said 'I am lying'.

If this is still not sufficiently sophisticated to convince you, consider this apparently correct paradox:

No class is a member of itself.

Therefore (since it follows that the class of classes that are not members of themselves is not a member of itself, and from this that the class of classes that are not members of themselves *is* a member of itself), at least one class is a member of itself.

Lightning Never Strikes Twice in the Same Spot

The fear of lightning felt by primitive peoples, animals, and children has led, like the fear of the unknown that has encouraged the spread of religion, to a whole host of mistaken notions which lie more in the realms of folklore and superstition than in the field of the popular fallacy. Perhaps the commonest fallacy is that lightning never strikes twice in the same place. However, the mast on the top of the Empire State Building was struck 68 times in the first ten years of its existence. Human beings are not very good conductors, but are struck roughly ten times as frequently as the laws of chance would indicate for the space they occupy.

Lightning is not a zig-zag in shape. The many photographs now available show that the old theory is wrong, and that lightning is most frequently in the form of a river, with tributaries; ball lightning, recorded but rare, is attested in *Nature* (June 1919, p. 284).

Among the fallacies exposed by Sir H. Spencer Jones, the then Astronomer Royal, in the *Daily Mail* of 16 September 1936, were the notions that if mirrors, scissors, knives or other bright objects, are covered (or curtains are drawn) the risk of lightning's striking is reduced.

Loch Ness Monsters

Since the discovery of the coelacanth, a 'fossil' still alive, I have been guilty of a bias towards the existence of a 'Loch Ness Monster'. However, the awesome *kraken* turned out to be a giant squid, and the continued failure decade after decade since 1933 to find physical evidence for such a monster's existence has been discouraging to 'believers'. Since 1961 the systematic scientific work performed by the Loch Ness Phenomenon Investigation Bureau has produced insufficient evidence to warrant a revision of Maurice Burton's *The elusive monster* (London, 1961).

Now comes a persuasive argument against the existence of a monster or monsters from Dr T. E. Thompson of the Department of Zoology, University of Bristol. In a recent personal communication he has written: "Unless 'Nessie' is presumed to be immortal, we should expect to find a breeding population of these monsters in the Loch. Such a population must consist of a sizeable number of individuals if it is to be stable; after all, ecologists express legitimate concern for large vertebrates such as rhinoceroses when their numbers fall below a hundred. It is impossible to believe that substantial numbers of large reptiles (as Nessie is usually claimed to be) could exist in the Loch without fairly frequent sightings. This objection is made the more cogent by the fact that reptiles (especially large reptiles) must breathe air at the surface.

94

Finally, one must remember that the Loch must have been frozen during the recent geological past, and so Nessie's ancestors must have entered the Loch after the subsequent thaw. By what route? There cannot be underground channels connecting the Loch with the sea, because the Loch would drain down to sea level if there were. There is no freshwater connexion to the sea ample enough to submerge even a small monster. And an overland route would be impossible for an aquatic vertebrate of the size and specialisation claimed".

Dr Thompson concludes: "The Loch Ness monster is based on superstitious nonsense. That the myth is perpetuated is largely the fault of opportunistic journalists, but it is regrettable that reputable scientists can occasionally be just as naughty. This is a pity because the general public already has difficulty in disentangling science fiction from science fact".

Lunatics *are Affected by Changes in the Moon (Latin:* luna)

We recall *Othello* (Act V, scene ii):

"It is the very error of the Moon;
She comes more nearer Earth than she was wont,
And makes men mad"

but it was already a common error among the Greeks that there was a connection between the changing moon and the periodically insane, that is to say, those who enjoy lucid intervals. Plutarch should not, therefore, have been puzzled by aristocratic Roman matrons who carried moon-amulets on their shoes to attract the lunacy-bearing moon-spirit so that it might enter the crescent charm and not its wearer.

Simple observation has helped to diminish the effect of this fallacy, though as always those who choose not to observe, and then to correlate their data with their assumptions, will continue to cherish the latter rather than the former.

M

Macbeth's Murder of Duncan was Unprecedented in Scottish Monarchical History

The Macbeth familiar to us all from Shakespeare's tragedy bears little or no resemblance to the figure known to historians from the documentary record.

Macbeth ruled from 1040–1057, a good span for a Scottish king in the Middle Ages. He was not regarded as a usurper, as is proved by the fact that he is buried on Iona, the restingplace of legitimate kings.

There were probably at least two attempts to deprive Macbeth of the throne, including those in 1046 and 1054 led by Siward of Northumbria. In 1054, Malcolm was apparently given possession of part of southern Scotland, and this may be the reason why some chroniclers believe Macbeth to have been killed in 1054. Macbeth was actually killed by Malcolm III in 1057, near Lumphanan in Mar and not in his own castle.

Neither did Macbeth kill Duncan in his own castle (Act II. iii. 11, *Lady Macbeth:* "Woe, alas! what, in our house?"). It was at 'the Smith's House' near Elgin.

Inevitably, most controversy centres on the bloodiness of the deed and the connivance of Lady Macbeth. There was probably no guilty Lady Macbeth of Scotland. Macbeth alone should be blamed, but for what?

Macbeth's murder of Duncan I was not an isolated act of butchery, but part of a traditional pattern, according to which a king was murdered by a successor of the alternate line. Thus, Dr Stones tells us, "Constantine (995–997) succeeded by the killing of Kenneth II, and was killed by his successor Kenneth III". Kenneth III was murdered by his successor, Malcolm II (1005–1034), Duncan's grandfather. Macbeth's murder of Duncan I, which has been so enormous in the public imagination, was neither more nor less savage than Malcolm III's murder of Macbeth.

'Mad as a Hatter' Refers to Madness or Hatters

Lewis Carroll with his penchant for linguistic games presumably knew perfectly well that his 'Mad Hatter' meant 'a venomous adder', but since his readers may have been misled by Tenniel's drawings, it should be pointed out that 'mad' meant 'venomous' and 'hatter' is a corruption of 'adder', or viper, so that the phrase 'mad as an atter' originally meant 'as venomous as a viper'.

'Mandarin' Is a Word of Chinese Origin

A mandarin is thought of as a high-ranking Chinese official, but the Chinese name for such an official is *kuan* and the word 'mandarin' derives ultimately from the Indo-European *man* (mind), giving *mantra* (counsel), *mantrin* (counsellor, minister) in Sanskrit, the Malay *mantri* and the Portuguese *mandarim* (the official) and *mandarino* (the language) from *mandar* (to command).

Marie-Antoinette *Said*
"If the Peasants Have No Bread, Let Them Eat Cake"

The quotation from the *Confessions* of Jean-Jacques Rousseau runs: "Enfin je me rappelai le pis-aller d'une grande princesse à qui l'on disait que les paysans n'avaient pas de pain, et qui répondit: 'Qu'ils mangent de la brioche' ". (I finally recalled the thoughtless aphorism of a great princess, to whom someone said that the peasants had no bread to eat, who replied 'Then let them eat cake'.)

It has always been assumed that it was Marie-Antoinette whom Rousseau pilloried in this manner, but that cannot be the case, for she arrived in France in 1770, some two years after Rousseau wrote the passage in question.

A **Martyr** *Is One Who Dies for a Belief*

This idea is very commonly believed, but it is only partly true. The Greek *martyr* means 'witness', and Skeat's definition is 'one who suffers for a belief': death is not a necessary part of the definition, though in religion a 'martyr' is generally taken to denote someone who died a heroic death rather than renounce a belief.

The Tolpuddle Martyrs, six Dorset labourers who suffered for their belief in trades unionism in the 1830s, were not executed but merely transported to Australia in 1834 and permitted to return before their seven years' sentence was up.

The Human Eye Can **Mesmerise** Wild Animals

By building up a relationship with certain animals, particularly the dog, human beings can affect their actions. They have no power at all over wild animals, or even over those domestic animals which choose not to obey, as cat-lovers will agree with alacrity. Francis Galton, in *Inquiries into human faculty and its development* (London, 1883), states that man "has no natural power at all over many other creatures. Who, for instance, ever succeeded in frowning away a mosquito, or in pacifying an angry wasp by a smile?"

Birds **Migrate** on the Same Day Each Year

Dozens of fallacies concerning bird migration can be found in standard works such as A. Landsborough Thompson's *Bird migration* (London, 1949) or J. Dorst's *Les migrations des oiseaux* (Paris, 1956), but it will be sufficient to explode one of the commonest which, despite regular scientific refutation by one ornithologist after another, recurs annually. According to Californian newspapers, the cliff swallows nesting at the San Juan Capistrano Mission there always leave the Mission on 23 October for their southward migration and return on 19 March, even taking account of leap years! The fact remains that their departure date varies from year to year.

Milk Turns Sour During a Thunderstorm

One of the many fallacies connecting two events together, when a third event is the cause of both.

Hot, humid weather favours *both* the occurrence of thunderstorms *and* rapid development of bacterial changes in milk producing the lactic acid which, at a certain point, turns milk sour. There is no necessary connection between the two phenomena which may be caused by sultry weather.

A Snake Cannot Kill a **Mongoose**

There is a theory that the mongoose is protected against snake-bite by eating a certain plant, thus obtaining a preventative antidote. This is not true. A mongoose can easily be killed by a snake if it does not immediately seize the snake behind the head to render it powerless and then break its backbone by biting it or cracking it like a whip. If the mongoose makes a mistake in this process, it can easily be bitten to death, an occurrence seen frequently in India.

If You Left a Crowd of **Monkeys** *Alone with Typewriters Long Enough They Would be Able to Recreate The Whole Works of Shakespeare*

This type of fallacy is normally used to ridicule the human faculty of creativity, particularly in the case of avant-garde writing or indeed any other literature which the reader is too lazy to appreciate.

Darrell Huff, author of the important exposure of statistical fallacies *How to lie with statistics* (London, 1954), has exploded this particular error in *How to take a chance* (London, 1960).

Random tapping of typewriter keys by one monkey would produce the initial 'd' of *dear sir* at the rate of one a minute; three monkeys over ten weeks could between them produce the word 'dear' with the letters in the right order; but to make the words 'dear sir' including the space in the right place would take 10,000 monkeys a hundred and fifty years. It is therefore inconceivable that any product of the human imagination could be replicated in any comparable way by random methods (which devalues among other examples the story *La biblioteca de Babel* by Jorge Luis Borges, in *Ficciones*).

Sir Arthur Eddington pointed the same moral in a limerick (though I am aware of the fallacy that 'all limericks are *ipso facto* true'):

> There once was a brainy baboon
> who always breathed down a bassoon,
> for he said "it appears
> that in billions of years
> I shall certainly hit on a tune".

The Contents of the **Moon** Fell on the Earth

Baron A. d'Espiard de Colonge is responsible, in his bizarre book *L'Égypte et l'Océanie* (Paris, 1882), for propagating a large number of fallacies.

The main error concerns the history of the Moon and the Earth, for the good Baron stated without a shred of proof that at some time the seas, continents and cities of the inhabited Moon fell to Earth, burying in the process the contemporary cities and valleys of the Earth in sand (where there was once flourishing life) and water (where there was once land). "Modern Europeans and all other peoples", he wrote excitedly, "have only a few centuries in which to organise and prepare on our Earth to withstand assaults from extra-terrestrial powers". He considered this inter-galactic warfare to be only one episode in universal carnage.

D'Espiard de Colonge argues that the sand covering much of Egypt is of lunar origin, and that the Pyramids as we see them today represent only one section of the ancient structures. In fact, he states, there are long galleries, tunnels, rooms, and treasure-houses of great antiquity. Initiates know where these tunnels are, and have access to them in the event of future wars.

It all sounds very thrilling, but the mundane archaeological fact of the matter is that the tunnels of d'Espiard do not exist.

Moths Eat Clothes

Not quite so simple. What actually happens is that clothes-moths lay eggs on cloth, and these eggs develop into larvae which then eat tiny particles of cloth. The larvae change into pupae, each forming a tiny cocoon, and after a time the fully-grown moths emerge from the cocoons. The adult moths do not eat cloth.

Black is the Colour of **Mourning**

White is the prevalent colour of mourning, particularly in the Far East, Ancient Rome, and Sparta. In England mourners wore white up until the Middle Ages, and Henry VIII is recorded as having worn it for Anne Boleyn (who wore *yellow* for Catherine of Aragon). Yellow is worn in Egypt and Burma. Deep blue was worn during the Republican Roman period. Greyish-brown is the traditional colour of mourning in Ethiopia and pale brown in Iran. Among the Celts and Gypsies the prevalent colour of mourning is red.

A **Mule** Is the Offspring of A She-ass and a Stallion

Not technically, no. A mule is the offspring of a he-ass and a mare. The correct name for the off-spring of a she-ass and a stallion is a hinny. Everyone asserts that a mule is incapable of giving birth, but the operative word is 'ordinarily', for cases have been known. And as for the legend of its stubbornness, let the *Oxford English Dictionary* defend the animal: "With no good grounds, the mule is a proverbial type of obstinacy."

Mumps in Men Causes Sterility

A team at a London hospital has published a study of nearly 200 men who had mumps in the five years before, and there was no evidence that the condition stopped them from fathering children.

Mussolini *Made the Italian* Trains
Run On Time

A common defence of Italian fascism was that regimentation and efficiency replaced an easy-going life and inefficiency. However, questioning of people who actually lived in Italy between the March on Rome (22 October 1922) and the execution at Como in 1945 bear witness to the fact that Italian railways were no more careful of timetables than they are today.

N

Napoleon I Was the First to Call England 'A **Nation of Shopkeepers**'

He merely quoted Adam Smith's *Wealth of nations* (London, 1776), having it first from Barère, who publicly used it of England in the French Convention of 11 June 1794, in allusion to Howe's battle of 1 June: "Let Pitt, then, boast of his victory to his nation of shopkeepers".

Adam Smith actually wrote, "To found a great empire for the sole purpose of raising up a people of customers, may at first sight appear a project fit only for a nation of shopkeepers. It is, however, a project altogether unfit for a nation of shopkeepers; but extremely fit for a nation that is governed by shopkeepers".

Napoleon's actual words were, "L'Angleterre est une nation de boutiquiers".

Nero *Fiddled While Rome Burned*

The violin was not invented until the 16th century, so that story must surely die soon. Was the instrument a lyre or lute-type then found in Rome? It is known that he played an instrument and also that he wrote poetry (Suetonius records having seen his notebooks with his own erasures), but he was at Antium when the fire that ruined half of Rome broke out in A.D. 64. The rumour that he had had the fire started began to circulate when he took the opportunity to build on the ashes his own colossal Domus Aurea. Nero himself put the blame on Christians, who were no more likely to have started the fire than he was.

Nests *are Used by Birds for Sleeping*

It has been observed that a mother bird will infrequently doze off while sitting on her eggs, but of course birds are as clean as pigs in their habits and leave their nests at dusk to sleep in tree branches. Town children often imagine birds asleep in their nests at night.

The **Nightingale,** *If She Should Sing*

"The nightingale, if she should sing by day,
When every goose is cackling, would be thought
No better a musician than the wren"

says Shakespeare in *The Merchant of Venice* (V, i), falling into the popular error of believing the singing nightingale to be the henbird. Only the cock nightingale can sing.

Nightingales *Sing Only at Night*

No known species of nightingale sings only by night, though both *Daulias luscinia* and *Daulias vera* (common in Britain) are more usually heard at night.

Nightmares *Are Connected with Mares*

The Old English 'maere' (incubus, a demon descending on you while you sleep, in the popular fancy) is the source of the second syllable in our familiar word for a bad dream, 'nightmare'. Related to the word 'maere' are the Polish *zmora,* the Czech *mura* (both meaning 'nightmare') and the first syllable of the Old Irish *Morrigain,* denoting the Queen of the Little People.

The modern English 'mare' is derived by contrast from the Old English 'mearh', meaning 'horse', and has no connection with 'maere' at all.

North American Indians *Used to Massacre White Pioneers*

At the time when Columbus 'discovered' America, there were just short of a million Indians in the area now known as the United States; the figure at the end of the 19th century was about a quarter of a million. At least a thousand massacres by white men are recorded, but in *The Gospel of the Red Man* (1939), Ernest Thompson Seton cannot identify a single massacre of whites by Indians.

There Are **Nuts** *in May*

On this fallacy depends the popular children's song "Here we go gathering nuts in May". As Brewer states in *A dictionary of phrase and fable,* the phrase "is a perversion of "Here we go gathering *knots of may*", referring to the old custom of gathering knots of flowers on May Day, or, to use the ordinary phrase, "to go a-maying". Of course there are no nuts to be gathered in May.

O

The Principle of **Occam's Razor** is that The Simplest Explanation is Best

William of Occam (or Ockham), who died about 1349, defended evangelical poverty as a Franciscan against Pope John XXII, and spent some time in prison at Avignon on a charge of heresy in 1328. In the popular mind, he is unfairly remembered for his enunciation of the principle of parsimony, or Occam's Razor, by which 'entities must not be unnecessarily multiplied'. The simplest explanation is the best provided but *only if* it covers all the known facts. Instead of reasoning from universal premises passed down from a higher authority, we should generalize from natural observations, a doctrine later espoused by Francis Bacon, Hobbes, and indeed all empiricists.

An **Octopus** Can Strangle a Man

Pure fantasy. It has been reported rarely that a swimmer has been held by one of the eight suckers of an octopus, but no harm has ever resulted, at least to the swimmer. Octopuses are also alleged to have bitten human beings with their beaklike mouths and to have injected venom, but no consequence has ever been more serious than a slight and temporary swelling.

Words Cannot Mean Their **Opposite**

For the student of words from the careful listing of Roget to the subtle imagination of Lewis Carroll, nothing is more enchanting than words in any language which mean their own opposite, something which is regularly believed by the unwary to be impossible.

Let formerly meant to prevent, as when Hamlet, intent on following his father's ghost, shouts at those who would stop him, "Unhand me, gentlemen. By heaven, I'll make a ghost of him that lets me!" Nowadays, he would say that he would make a ghost of anyone who would *not* let him follow his father's spectre.

Scan means to scrutinize with great care; or to glance so briefly that one takes in the headlines or main points only. For instance, "The bibliographer scanned the first edition carefully to ensure that it was perfect in every detail", and "The traveller barely scanned the front page before handing the magazine to his wife".

Shame*ful* and shame*less* are virtually the same thing; so are valuable and *in*valuable. *Nice* in mediaeval usage meant 'foolish, dull, strange, or stupid'. I can *distract* (entertain) a reader without, I hope, *distracting* him (sending him out of his wits).

An **Orphan** *Is Parentless*

It is often stated that an orphan is one who has lost both father and mother, but the *Shorter Oxford Dictionary* defines 'orphan' as 'one deprived by death of father or mother', so that a child with one parent still living should properly be referred to as an orphan.

113

Ostrich Wings are Useless, as the Bird Cannot Fly

The ostrich cannot fly, but uses its wings to turn sharply when eluding a hunter. Ostriches can both jump and swim.

Ostriches Bury Their Heads in the Sand

This curious fallacy probably arose from the observation that, when sighting danger from afar, they occasionally drop to the ground with their necks parallel to the ground and watch intently. Then, if danger approaches, they do what every other animal with strong legs is likely to do: they run like hell.

President Woodrow Wilson is only one of a thousand politicians and orators who have used the picturesque figure of speech, obviously thinking it a fact and not a fallacy. In a speech on 1 February 1916 he declared: "America cannot be an ostrich with its head in the sand". To which one is tempted to add "neither can an ostrich", for it would quickly suffocate.

Ostriches Can Digest Coins and Keys

Metallic and other hard substances are taken into the gizzard by ostriches, much as common fowl take small sharp pebbles, but they are not digested, despite Shakespeare:

"Ah, villain, thou wilt betray me, amd get a thousand crowns of the king by carrying my head to him; but I'll make thee eat iron like an ostrich, and swallow my sword

114

like a great pin, ere thou and I part" (Jack Cade to Alexander Iden)—*King Henry VI*, Part 2 (IV, x).

But the fallacy that such metal objects are actually digested by ostriches was repudiated by Sir Thomas Browne in *Pseudodoxia epidemica* (London, 1646), Book III, chapter 22:

> "The common opinion of the Ostrich, Struthiocamelus, or Sparrow Camel, conceives that it digesteth iron, and this is confirmed by the affirmations of many: besides swarms of others, Rhodiginus in his prelections taketh it for granted, Johannes Langius in his epistles pleadeth experiment for it; the common picture also confirmeth it, which usually describeth this animal with an horseshoe in its mouth. Notwithstanding, upon inquiry we find it very questionable, and the negative seems most reasonably entertained . . ."

Ostriches eat vegetables and grass in the wild; in captivity according to the London Regent's Park Zoo they will eat almost anything, from meat to keys and coins, but of course they cannot *digest* these latter. Cuvier shall have the last word: "The powers of digestion in this bird are certainly very great, but their operation is confined to matters of an alimentary character".

An **Ovation** Is a Major Triumph

The popular press frequently refers to an ovation accorded to a figure deserving of every reward. But the Latin *ovatio* is, to quote Cassell's *Latin dictionary* (1948 printing) merely "a kind of lesser triumph in which the victorious general proceeded to the Capitol on horseback or on foot". An ovation is thus a secondary triumph.

P

The *'Panama' Hat* Comes From the Central American State of Panama

A Panama hat is one made from the undeveloped leaves of the stemless screw-pine (*Carloduvica palmata*) and has nothing to do with the nation of Panama.

Parrots Can Live to be a Hundred

Not so far as the experts have been able to obtain reliable records. Hundred-year-old parrots certainly belong in the realm of the fable; nevertheless a raven in captivity reached an age of 69 years.

St. Patrick Was an Irishman

St. Patrick (385 ?–461 ?) seems to have been born near the west coast somewhere between the Clyde and the Severn estuary, but in any case not in Ireland. A Romano-Briton, he merely *evangelized* the Irish, but of course there were Christians in Ireland long before Patrick began to preach the Gospel there. The Irish bishop of the time was Palladius.

A *Pedagogue* Originally Meant a Teacher

The Greek *paidagogos* was "a slave who led a boy to school, *hence* [my italics], a tutor, instructor", and not

118

originally the boy's teacher. It was in Latin that *paedagogus* came to mean "a preceptor", and this usage passed into French and other modern languages with its changed meaning.

St. Peter's *Is the Cathedral of Rome*

A widespread fallacy, accounting for the fact that when I last visited St. John Lateran (San Giovanni in Laterano) in Rome it was almost completely deserted, though it is in fact not only the Cathedral of Rome, and the Metropolitan Church of its bishops, but "Mother and head of all churches in the city and the world" as its façade inscription pronounces ('omnium urbis et orbis ecclesiarum mater et caput').

Sir Paul Harvey's *Oxford Companion to English Literature* (entry PETER'S, St., Rome) perpetuates the error of calling the Vatican church 'the metropolitan church of the Roman see'.

Homing **Pigeons** *Have an Unerring Instinct for Returning to Their Point of Origin over Hundreds of Miles*

Common knowledge, indeed. But not to anyone who has had to train a homing pigeon, beginning from ten feet. Rewards are given to the pigeon for each success, and not for each failure. A homing pigeon cannot be taken completely out of sight of any known landmark and expected to return, so its 'instinct' is in fact simply the use of a visual memory. This is assisted by careful breeding of the birds with the best proven memories. As for the ability of *carrier pigeons*, the U.S. Army Signal Corps (the largest breeder and trainer of carrier pigeons) does not expect its best birds to return over a distance exceeding twenty-five miles, and then only after repeated training flights over the same territory.

In Architecture, the Terms *'Pillar"* and *'Column'* are Interchangeable

How many popular writers on travel and famous buildings can tell the difference between a column and a pillar? A column is always cylindrical in plan. A pillar, on the other hand, need not be cylindrical in plan. The two words are used interchangeably in hundreds of major reference works, including for example Arnold Whittick's *Symbols* (2nd ed., London, 1971).

"Play It Again, Sam"

One of the most evocative lines from any film, quoted above from Humphrey Bogart's famous scene in the 1943 film *Casablanca*, directed by Michael Curtiz, refers to the song 'As Time Goes By', by M. K. Jerome and Jack Scholl.

The trouble is that Bogart never said it. I awaited the line with bated breath on a recent showing of the movie, and can confirm that the line really runs, "Play it, Sam".

Marco *Polo* Wrote a History
Of His Travels to the East

Only in the figurative sense; the man who actually *wrote* Marco Polo's narrative of his adventures was a certain Rustichiello or Rusticiano of Pisa, who was in jail with Polo in 1298–1299 after the victory of the Genoese over the Venetians in Curzola Bay. The original text as dictated seems to have been in *French*, however, not in the Venetian dialect, and the first printed edition appeared in *German* in 1477.

Was There a '*Pope Joan*'?

A scandalous story, still widely believed, alleges that in 855, between the pontificates of Leo IV and Benedict III, a woman was unanimously elected Pope. The philosopher Leibniz lent his support to the following absurd tale. A young Englishwoman called Joan, born at Ingelheim near Mainz, travelled in a monk's habit from Fulda to Athens, and later in Rome so delighted churchmen by her learning that, still in male attire, she became known as 'the Roman wonder'. After being elected pope, she had an affair with her valet, which came to light when, in the course of a procession from the Colosseum to the church of S. Clemente, she gave birth to a child and died. Friedrich Gontard, who writes of Pope Joan in *Die Päpste* (Munich, 1959), suggests that "the fable probably originated in the tenth century when, over a period of sixty-seven years, each pope was more sinister, more worthless, and more dangerous than the one before him". The story continued to obtain credence until the 16th century, for the tradition says that every Pope up to Leo X (1513–1521) had to undergo a sex test. At the enthronement ceremony an antique chair with an open seat (the *sella stercoraria*) was occupied by the newly-elected Pope; after due examination a deacon called out *Habet!* ('He has'), whereupon the people of Rome chorussed *Deo gratias!* ('Thanks be to God!').

A papal bust of 'John VIII, a woman from England' in Siena Cathedral was renamed 'Pope Zachary' by Pope Clement VIII (1592–1605). See also Lawrence Durrell's amusing novel on the non-existent woman, *Pope Joan*, which of course merely had the effect of reawakening the popular fallacy that such a pope had once existed.

The **Pores** of the Skin 'Breathe'

'Wash with our soap and let your pores breathe' run the popular advertisements by soap manufacturers who should know better and probably do.

Vilhjalmur Stefansson exploded this fallacy in *The standardisation of error* (1928), but of course the error remains standard: "The skin does not excrete any appreciable amount of harmful substances from the body, nor do the pores 'breathe'. Therefore your system is not purified by 'keeping the pores open' ". Stefansson goes on to defy the three-baths-a-day-fanatics: "A chief function of the skin is to protect the body; poisons, such as mercury, will not penetrate if the skin is oiled with its own secretions, but will penetrate if the natural lubricants have been washed away with warm water, soap, or other methods . . ."

122

It is Bad Grammar to End a Sentence With a **Preposition**

It would instead be accurate to state that "if it is possible to end a sentence less awkwardly than with a preposition, the preposition should be avoided". But it would sometimes be much more awkward to avoid the preposition. What about this sentence, culled from a war-time *Reader's Digest*?

> "Little Tommy, ill upstairs, complained to his mother as she sat down to read to him: 'What did you bring that book I didn't want to be read to out of up for?' "
>
> "It is a good rule to go by" is a better sentence than the clumsy "It is a good rule by which to go".

Pride *Goes Before a Fall*

'Pride goeth before a raise', wrote Ogden Nash, and his sly aphorism at the expense of the Old Testament (Proverbs, xvi, 18) was as mistaken as the supposed original, 'Pride goeth (or goes) before a fall'. The Latin version of the Hebrew original familiar since the Middle Ages runs "Contritionem praecedit superbia: et ante ruinam exaltatur spiritus", which might be rendered "Pride goes before contrition, and hauteur before destruction". The popular misreading eliminates the crucial fourth, fifth, sixth and seventh words of the above translation.

Printing from Moveable Type
Was Invented by Gutenberg

In the *Novum Organon*, Francis Bacon attributed the invention of printing, gunpowder and the magnet to 'the moderns', by implication Europeans. J. B. Bury, in his *Idea of progress* (London, 1920), writing three centuries later than Bacon, awards the 'Moderns' the palm over the 'Ancients' precisely for those three inventions.

"Yet nowhere in his book", complains Joseph Needham, "is there even a footnote pointing out that none of the three was of European origin". Printing, gunpowder, and the magnet, were all invented by the Chinese.

As late as 1952, writing in *The Times*, the then Keeper of Oriental Books and Manuscripts in the British Museum stated that, while block-printing was known and used in 8th-century China, it was left to Europeans to devise printing with moveable types.

"This is of course nonsense", observes Dr Needham. The first known user of moveable types was "Pi Sheng *(fl. c.* A.D. 1060), who used porcelain or earthenware, while the Koreans were doing a good deal of printing with copper or bronze founts at the end of the fourteenth century, i.e. well before the time of Gutenberg. Yet the Museum of Printing at Mainz contains no reference to the Chinese inventions, and organizers of commemorative exhibitions in our own country have generally been loth to acknowledge them".

Pyramids of Egypt

The best-known pyramids of Egypt have occupied the imagination of cranks of many countries for several centuries, and no attempt is made here to summarize the numerous occult and pseudo-scientific interpretations of these funerary monuments. All known pyramids contain or have once contained sarcophagi, and most bear the names of the kings buried within them. The pyramid of Cheops was *not* an astronomical observatory-cum-table of measurement which can be interpreted as a chronological guide to the principle events of past and future history. The methods of planning and construction are known in outline, if not in full detail, and are adequately published in I. E. S. Edwards' *The Pyramids of Egypt* (1947), though it was W. M. Flinders Petrie, in *The Pyramids and Temples of Gizeh* (London, 1883), who first proved that all the pyramids were intended and used as tombs.

One important fallacy still prevalent was first propounded by Richard Lepsius, who suggested that their size corresponded to the length of their owner's reign: this is known as the 'accretion theory'. It is odd that it should have been suggested at all, since all one needs to refute it is a chronology of Pharaonic Egypt together with a tape measure. Thus, the pyramid of Pepi II (who reigned for 94 years) should have become several times as large as that of Mykerinos, who reigned for about 18 years. In fact, the considerations involved were probably the ruler's inclination, power, and religious beliefs.

Q

Quicklime Destroys a Corpse

Some writers of detective stories still labour under the odd delusion that quicklime will 'eat' a dead body, and it helped to convict the multiple murderess Mrs Belle Gunness of La Porte, Indiana, whose fourteen victims were excellently preserved in the tell-tale substance.

Quicksands Suck in Human Beings

So do rivers, come to that, but quicksands (a mixture of sand and water) will support the human body much more easily than water unmixed with sand. A sucking sound that panicking victims fear is made only when a large object or person is pulled *out* of a quicksand. The force creating the suction is in the puller, not in the quicksand or bog, or whatever the quagmire may be. The danger lies simply in exhausting oneself by struggling; those who do not struggle seldom sink below the armpits.

So don't panic. If you sense you are getting into a quicksand, lie down and *roll* across it. If it should be too soft to roll on, lie on your back with your mouth as high as possible. The quicksand is denser than your body, and so your body cannot sink completely into it.

R

A *Rabbit* Should be Picked Up by the Ears

Merely because a rabbit's ears are relatively large, it does not follow that rabbits should be picked up by their ears, as the popular theory goes. They should be picked up by the skin behind the shoulders, as guinea-pigs should. Cats should be lifted below the front part of the body, with the back legs resting on your arm. Geese or swans should be picked up by the wings just behind the back, never by the delicate legs. Small cage-birds such as canaries should be enclosed in the hand from the back, taking care not to grip them too tightly.

Railways Were Built for Trains

A virtually ubiquitous fallacy. The steam locomotive had not been invented when the first wooden railways were laid. Their purpose was to run trucks of coal from the pithead to the harbour for transportation. Such railways were first used in 1602 at Newcastle-upon-Tyne, England. It was not until 1820 that iron was used for train-tracks, and not until 1857 that iron was replaced by steel.

Sir Walter *Raleigh* Laid Down His Cloak in the Mire for Elizabeth I

An example of a romantic idea perpetuated until it forms part of the national consciousness. The anecdote has no foundation in fact; it was invented by worthy Thomas Fuller (1608–1661) and repeated by Sir Walter Scott in his popular novel *Kenilworth* (1821).

'Re' Is an Abbreviation of 'Referring to' or 'Regarding'

A commercial letter might begin: "Re. your communication of yesterday's date . . ." This is often taken to mean "Regarding your communication . . ." hence the full stop after re. But *re* is not an abbreviation, and should be italicised (or underlined) as a foreign word. It is the ablative form of the Latin word *res*, meaning 'matter', 'thing', or 'affair', and in business means 'in the matter of . . .'

'Red' Square in Moscow was So Called After the Russian Revolution

The name *krasniy* ('red', 'beautiful'), was applied to Moscow's Red Square long before the Bolshevik October Revolution of 1917, and has therefore nothing to do with the 'East is Red' slogan or the 'Red Flag' motif.

Incidentally, it is another common fallacy that there was only one revolution. There had been dozens of Russian revolutions prior to the Bolshevik victory, one of the most notable being the 1905 Revolution, which began with the Bloody Sunday massacre of 9 January (or 22 January, the Old-Style Russian Calendar being thirteen days behind the Gregorian Calendar of the West up to February 1918). Another error is to believe that St. Petersburg changed its name to Lenin-

131

grad. In fact, St. Petersburg changed its name in 1914 to Petrograd, and only from 1924 became Leningrad.

The 'White' **Rhinoceros** Is White

Both 'black' and 'white' rhinoceroses are grey-brown in colour. The term 'white' is a corruption of the Afrikaans word *wijd*, which means 'wide', and refers to the animal's lips. The 'black' rhinoceros is distinguishable by its pointed upper lip, used for browsing on thorny bushes, while the white rhinoceros feeds on grass. The rhinoceros' horn does not have a bony core, despite the common assumption: it consists of keratin, the material of which human fingernails are composed.

Rice-Paper Is Made from Rice

Rice-paper is not made from rice, but derives from the pith of the so-called rice-paper plant whose scientific name is *Aralia* or *Fatsia Papyrifera*.

Indian **Rope-Trick**

The 'Indian rope-trick' is claimed to be a conjuring performance in which a small boy climbs a rope in full view of an audience *in the open air* and then disappears. The feat has been replicated on stage easily enough by means of ladders, mirrors, special lighting, and/or light-absorbing material for the boy's clothes.

Other variants are the use of a 'rope' consisting of jointed bamboo rods, or the substitution of a monkey dressed in turban and *dhoti* for the boy.

But no Western (or indeed Eastern) conjuror has been able to repeat the stage feat in the open air, as has so often been claimed by the gullible. Lord Northbrook, Viceroy of India, offered £10,000 in 1875 to anyone who would demonstrate the Indian rope-trick. Though the offer was widely advertised, no claimant came forward.

S

The *Sahara* Region of Northern Africa
Is Perennially Dry

Though the North African desert is, outside the Polar Regions, the least-populated area of the globe, with fewer than two million inhabitants, there is archaeological and even more abundant geological evidence that the 'desert' was once more fertile and even now possesses seven major water regions of underground water reservoirs totalling an estimated 15,000,000 million cubic metres of groundwater. This figure is increasing by some 4,000 million cubic metres a year by the acquisition of rainwater running underground from the desert's fringe areas towards the central rockbound aquifers.

Salad Days are the Happiest Days
of One's Youth

Not so! Despite the nostalgic musical play by Sandy Wilson 'salad days' are the gauche, anxious, lonely days recalled by Cleopatra in Shakespeare's *Anthony and Cleopatra* (I,v), when she remembers that her youthful days were 'salad' days because she loved badly, like a salad, green and cold. The implication is entirely pejorative: 'salad days' look forward to a maturity which is expected to be far more enjoyable.

Sandwiches were Invented by
the Fourth Earl of Sandwich (1718–1792)

No! The compulsive English gambler certainly ate cooked meat between two slices of bread at the tables rather than leave them for an elaborate cooked meal, but the Romans had introduced the idea throughout their Empire seventeen centuries earlier.

Sap Rises

In the spring it is believed in the folklore that sap 'rises', and likewise in the autumn that it 'falls'. But in fact sap moves from the centre of the tree to the bark and back—never up or down.

To **Scan** a Page is to Glance Through it Perfunctorily

Nowadays we often hear of someone who had not enough time to read a book properly: he confesses that he merely *scanned* it. To the extent that it is a widespread meaning, it must be correct, for the English language recognises no academy or official dictionary (despite the high status generally accorded to the *Oxford English Dictionary*). But if one remembers that a gunner *scans* the horizon for any sign of the enemy even now, then we must recall the original meaning, which was to scrutinise carefully, to examine point by point, to look at all parts intently.

*"Great **Scott!**" Derives from Sir Walter Scott*

The exclamation "Great Scott!" derived from the United States General Winfield Scott (1786–1866), a notoriously fussy candidate for the presidency in 1852. Scott failed in his bid, but he has a greater—if unwanted—significance as the origin of a popular phrase.

*Drinking **Sea Water** Causes Madness*

People can go mad from thirst (and starvation), and shipwreck survivors who drink sea water will aggravate their thirst, hence the connection of two ideas in reality unconnected. A man requires a minimum of 800 c.c. of water a day (W. S. S. Ladell in *Nature*, 25 March 1944, p. 385), and if there is a shortfall of 200 c.c., then that amount of sea water can be added to the fresh water with beneficial results.

*William **Shakespeare** Used a Vocabulary Much Greater than that Useable Today*

Quite the contrary. The English language has grown enormously since Elizabethan times. Webster's unabridged dictionary of 1934 listed over 600,000 words, while the 3rd ed. of 1961 cut the 'unabridged' [sic] to a mere 450,000. It is reckoned that more than a million words in present-day English have not yet become obsolete, whereas, according to Irving J. Lee (in *Language habits in human affairs*, New York, 1941), Shakespeare used fewer "than twenty thousand different words in his plays". The average vocabulary of the contemporary English-speaker is certainly lower than that of Shakespeare, but writers and others of high literacy can make use of a lexicon far in excess of that useable by our greatest playwright.

Sharks Frequently Attack and Eat Men

Human cowardice must be responsible, together with the usual barrel-load of scientific ignorance and refusal to shake off old prejudices, for this fallacy, recently revitalized by the best-selling novel and film *Jaws*. Actual cases of men being attacked by sharks are so rare that the U.S. Navy's Bureau of Aeronautics thought it worth stating in the pamphlet *Shark sense* (1944) that "there is practically no danger that an unwounded man floating in a life-jacket will be attacked by a shark". A foremost expert, Captain William E. Young, wrote in *Shark! Shark!* (New York, 1933) that he had never known of a shark's attacking a living man, though he thought it might happen. Bergen Evans concludes his remarks on this fallacy in *The natural history of nonsense* (London, 1947, p. 81): "Of the several hundred varieties of sharks only half a dozen have the denture necessary for man-eating, and of these not all have the disposition. Of those that have, few get the opportunity, and of those, few make the most of it".

'Sirloin' was Originally So Called by King James I

In a 1978 television programme, the owner of a certain British stately home claimed proudly that it was in his home that James I had jokingly dubbed an excellent helping of beef 'Sir Loin'.

Actually 'surloin' (the preferred, though less common spelling) comes from the 14th-century French word *surlonge* (the upper part of a loin of beef), and it occurs as 'surloyn' as early as the reign of Henry VI in the accounts of the Ironmongers' Company.

Snake Fallacies

1. The American puff adder is venomous. It is not, unlike the dreaded African puff adder. The American puff adder has to use its puff to frighten enemies and hypnotise prey.
2. Cobras can be 'charmed' by a snake-charmer. Snakes sense vibrations on the ground rather than 'hear' as human beings can hear, for they have no ears. It may look as though the cobra is being charmed by a flute's sound, but in fact the cobra is merely swaying in tune with the flute to get into a striking position! The charmer has sufficient skill to keep out of striking distance, or he never lives to see another day.
3. St. Patrick drove the snakes out of Ireland. There are quite a number of islands without snakes, but one does not have to allocate a saint to each in order to account for that fact!
4. Rattlesnakes always rattle before they strike. No: Dr A. I. Ortenburger of the University of Oklahoma

studied this habit among Arizona rattlesnakes, and found that only 4 percent of those he collected did in fact rattle before they struck.

5. Rattlesnakes add one rattle each year, so their age can be determined by counting their rattles. You're mixing them up with rings on a tree. A rattle is added each time the snake sheds its skin, but the frequency of shedding skin depends not on the calendar but on the amount of food it eats. It may shed its skin less frequently than annually, or four or five times in a year: the average is two or three times. But even if you know how well the snake has eaten, you might still guess wrongly, because rattles frequently break off.

6. Snakes coil round a tree. Painters and cartoonists often depict this scene, but it is entirely fallacious. A snake climbs a tree with its whole body extended in a straight line, gripping the trunk or branch with its expanded ribs and clinging with the concave rows of pointed scales as it presses against the bark. At rest, too, it clings to the upper surface of a branch, and does not coil round.

The Defeat of the **Spanish Armada**
Led to the Decline of Spain

This idea is believed and taught even now in many schools and colleges, but was dispatched fairly definitively in Garrett Mattingly's *The Armada* (Boston, 1959). Some scholars suggested that the defeat of the Spanish Armada in 1588 caused the decline of Spain and the rise of the British Empire. As Mattingly observes, "it is hard to see why they think so. By 1603, Spain had not lost to the English a single overseas outpost, while the English colonization of Virginia had been postponed for the duration".

To those who argue that the defeat of the Armada transferred control of the seas from Spain to Britain, Mattingly replies that before 1588, "English sea power in the Atlantic had usually been superior to the combined strengths of Castile and Portugal, and so it continued to be, but after 1588 the margin of superiority diminished. The defeat of the Armada was not so much the end as the beginning of the Spanish navy". To those who argue, on the other hand, that defeat dislocated the Spanish economy by the disruption of communications with America, Mattingly retorts "More treasure reached Spain in the years between 1588 and 1603 than in any other fifteen years in Spanish history".

In English **Spelling**, 'I' Comes Before 'E', Except After 'C'

Generation after generation of schoolchildren have been taught the above spelling rule, which works with 'field' and 'ceiling' perfectly well, but it is not a valid *rule*. 'Seize' and 'leisure' are only two of the many examples which test the 'rule' and find it so wanting that it had better be forgotten completely. Now.

The More Nuts a **Squirrel** Hoards, The Severer the Winter Will Be

The more nuts a squirrel hoards, the better the nut-season has been! The old country adage is completely false, as is the idea that all squirrels hibernate completely. Some squirrels hibernate completely, taking no food the whole time; the majority doze for days at a time, and take food at intervals when they wake; and others, especially in the mildest winters, do not go into a torpid state at all, remaining active, and feeding on bark and twigs as normal. During the Autumn they devour more food than is necessary, the store of fat being gradually consumed while the animals are asleep.

In **Statistics,** Every 'One Chance in a Hundred' Must Occur Once in Every Hundred Occasions

No subject except religion occasions more fallacious beliefs than statistics. If 'on average' an event occurs once in every hundred events, and the sample covers a thousand events, then that event may occur ten times in ten events, as long as no further event occurs in the other 990 events. Similarly, it may occur not at all in the first hundred, two hundred, or even nine hundred chances and yet still occur 'on average' once in a hundred events.

Sterility in Men Can Be Caused By
Close-Fitting Underpants Or
By Thermal Underwear

"Many infertile couples have been 'cured' by the advice to the man to give up tight underpants", writes J. Cohen in *Reproduction* (London, 1977).

Dr T. E. Thompson writes in refutation of this widespread fallacy: "At present there is no sound evidence that the style of underwear worn by a man (unless it actually induces morbidity) can influence his fertility.

The supposed scientific basis of the tale derives from laboratory studies that have established that heat produces detrimental effects on the functioning of the testis. But it is equally well established (see Cockett and Urry's *Male infertility, workup, treatment and research*, New York, 1977) that cold stress may harm the functioning of the testis. No mammalian organ system will continue to function properly if subjected to extreme temperature stress: this is not a peculiarity of the testis.

Further experimental information has been provided by a survey of the effects of deliberately excessive exposure of a team of volunteer students of medicine to the Finnish sauna bath. Twelve subjects used the sauna eight times in two weeks, the temperature in the bath being 77–90°C, considerably above the normal body-temperature which rarely reaches 40°C. The total sperm count was studied for a period of two months after the period of exposure to the high temperature of the sauna. The only deleterious effect noted was that a negligible drop in sperm counts occurred between the 30th and 39th days after the beginning of the experiment. The truth of the matter is that the blood circulation of the body, which penetrates the testis just as it does nearly all the other organs of the mammal, is ample to smooth out local fluctuations in the temperature of individual organs. The testis is little more at risk in the sauna than is the nose or the pancreas".

The Last **Straw** Breaks the Laden Camel's Back

Charles Dickens quoted this absurd fallacy in *Dombey and Son* (ch.2, 1848), without realising that no camel ever rose from its haunches with a burden too heavy to carry. Camels are too cautious to be overloaded, and will lie down until some of the unfair weight has been removed.

The regular load of a camel is 400 pounds, but H. E. Cross states that before World War I the natives of the Raj loaded their camels with up to 800 pounds and big camels in good condition have been known to carry 960 without excessive discomfort.

Succulents Need Little or No Water

"The old idea that cacti [and other succulents] need little or no water dies hard, but this is far from true", write Edgar and Brian Lamb in their *Pocket encyclopaedia of cacti in colour* (Poole, 1969). "Cacti may be able to go without water for a considerable period without looking too unhappy, but they enjoy a 'good drink' as much as most other plants. Even so, we find with the many growers we meet each year that there is still a general tendency to under-water rather than over-water. Another mistaken idea is that cacti should only be watered at the base, and never from above; after all, rain falls directly on and around species growing in the wild!"

Walther Haage confirms this view in his *Cacti and succulents* (London, 1963). "After all", he writes, "no plant, not even the most drought-resisting, can exist without any water for long".

Syphilis was Imported to the Old World From the New

This fallacy is so prevalent that it recurs in the otherwise entirely reputable *Penguin medical encyclopedia* (2nd ed., 1976): "There are no recognizable accounts of syphilis earlier than about A.D. 1500, but after the return of Columbus from the New World the disease spread as a plague from the Mediterranean across Europe. *Nobody can prove that Columbus and his men imported syphilis* (my italics), but it seems likely". In fairness to Peter Wingate, he does immediately confess that "There is, however, a considerable weight of contrary opinion, some of it well informed".

The problem is one of nomenclature, since the name 'syphilis' was not coined until 1530 (by Fracastorius, in his poem *Syphilis, sive Morbus Gallicus*), when it was fancifully derived from an unfortunate shepherd, one Syphilus, who cursed the sun during a heatwave and was punished with the 'new' disease.

Numerous characters in history have had what one might assume to have been syphilis if only the name had been applied earlier: Herod, king of the Jews, is said to have died of a malignant disease of the genitals, and the same applies to John of Gaunt (d. 1408).

T

How to Make Your Wife *Talk in Her Sleep*

The 16th-century Neapolitan prodigy Giambattista della Porta lived in a period, like the present, when the sciences were being attacked as reactionary by pseudo-scientists. Whereas the 20th-century scientist is subjected to irrational claims from those who claim experimental validity for parapsychology and flying saucers, the 16th-century seeker after truth was assailed by those claiming the reality of alchemy, prophecy, and witchcraft.

Della Porta was not a charlatan, but was taken in by alleged miracles. His field was optics, and he was easily led astray by claims for extraordinary discoveries in fields other than his own. Della Porta's *Magiae naturalis, sive de miraculis rerum naturalium libri iiii* (Naples, 1558) contains so many more 'miracles' than 'natural things' that one could effortlessly produce *A Dictionary of Common Fallacies* consisting solely (and uncharitably) of his own mistakes. The *Magiae naturalis* went into dozens of editions, and became one of the most widely-read books of the time. An English translation, *Natural magick* (London, 1658), shows that its attractions were not confined to southern Europe, and to those who could read Latin. "How to force a woman to babble in her sleep whatever we desire to know of her secrets" is a technique that perhaps the English language did not need to acquire. Della Porta advises the curious reader to wait until his wife is sound asleep, and then to place over her heart the tongue of a frog or of a wild duck, for these animals 'give tongue' at night! After waiting for the magic to take its effect, one asks the questions to be answered. If your wife does not answer at once, wait and repeat the questions. Ultimately, all will be revealed.

150

Tarantula Spiders *Spin Webs And are Highly Venomous*

While most spiders spin webs, the four-inch long tarantula cannot; it depends on its sting to kill small insects, but its venom is not a serious threat to human beings.

The Bite of the Tarantula *Spider Can Only Be Cured by Dancing the Tarantella*

A hysterical malady, tarantism, characterised by an impulse to dance, was common in Apulia (southern Italy) from the 15th to the 18th centuries. The city of Taranto was particularly connected with outbreaks of tarantism, which by folk etymology was confused with *Lycosa tarantula*, a spider found in the Taranto area. Confusion was so rife at one time that some thought that the dance was a cure for the spider's venomous bite, and others that the dance was *caused* by a bite! The tarantula spider is, however, entirely unconnected with the phenomenon of tarantism, which recurred in patients summer after summer.

Tarantula spiders still exist in the Taranto region, as does the tarantella dance. The playwright Oliver Goldsmith (in *Animated nature)* described the hoax played on visitors by the Tarantese. For a fee paid by a credulous traveller, a peasant would be 'bitten' by a spider, simulate collapse, and then be restored to health by the music and dancing of the tarantella. The 'explanation' of the Tarantese was that the sweating caused by dancing exuded the poison of the spider's bite!

William **Tell** Shot an Arrow
Through an Apple on His Son's Head

A stone in the Washington monument in the United States, contributed by the Swiss Government, bears the inscription, "This block is from the original chapel built to William Tell, in 1338, on Lake Lucerne, Switzerland, at the spot where he escaped from Gessler".

The Historical Society of Switzerland has diffidently pointed out to both governments concerned that both Tell and Gessler are wholly fictional characters, but the common fallacy persists. As long ago as August 1890 the canton of Schwyz ordered the Tell legend to be expunged (as nonhistorical) from the cantonal school textbooks. The events are usually placed in the 14th century and are first found in writings of the 15th century. Similar legends of marksmen shooting at an object on the head of a man or child are found in many countries, notably in England (William of Cloudesley) and Norway (Egil).

Setting the **'Thames'** on Fire

This common error began circulation when the name 'temse' was changed to 'sieve'. A labourer working with a sieve (or temse) would be urged to shake it so vigorously that the sparks would fly from it, and one exercising too little effort would be rebuked: "You'll never set the temse on fire". It is only comparatively recently that the nonsense 'Thames' element crept in.

Toads Are Connected with **Toadstools**

Dr Werner Broch writes from Basle that, among the various fallacies connected with toads in volume 1, I omitted their spurious connection with toadstools. Dr Broch reminds us that *Tod* is the German for 'death' and *Stuhl* the German for 'chair' or 'seat', thus bringing together with some force the poisonous nature of the fungus, which the English 'toadstool', comically omits. The Early English origin is 'todestole'.

The modern German word for the toadstool is *der Giftschwamm*, literally 'the poison fungus'.

Toads Do Harm in a Garden, and Tortoises Good

Toads are good for a garden, because they are insectivorous, and especially like to eat slugs and snails. Tortoises do not, and though often bought for their ability to keep down garden pests, are in fact exclusively herbivorous. It is possible that black beetles avoid them if possible, and consequently leave the garden of their own volition when tortoises are brought in, but there appears to be little evidence on this question either way.

Heinrich Schliemann Discovered Homeric **Troy**

No: the city excavated by Schliemann from 1870 to 1873 was the pre-Achaean city, long antecedent to any Troy known in Homeric times. But the site, Hissarlik, was the correct one, as predicted in Schliemann's extraordinarily percipient *Ithaka, der Peloponnes und Troja* of 1869. His *Trojanische Alterthümer* (Leipzig, 1874) appeared in the year that Schliemann started the equally fruitful campaign at Mycenae, on the Greek mainland.

It was Schliemann's successor Dörpfeld, working with money endowed by Schliemann, who finally uncovered the walls of the sixth stratum at Troy (contemporary with the height of the Mycenaean excavations) which Schliemann had wrongly believed to be Lydian.

Turkeys *Originated in Turkey*

Turkey-fowl originated wholly in the American continent, and were first imported into Europe shortly after the first invaders entered Mexico in 1518. However, they were confused at that time with the guinea-fowl which entered Europe from Africa via the Turkish colonies (Eric Partridge makes the same error in his *Origins*, 4th ed., London, 1966) and when the two species were subsequently differentiated, it was—inevitably perhaps in a world so inclined to error—the *American* bird which acquired the designation 'turkey'.

Increasing a Figure by **200%** *Doubles the Figure*

Stuart Campbell of Edinburgh kindly submits the popular fallacy that a sum increased by 200 percent is *tripled,* not doubled, as many assume without bothering to work it out. The initial 100 percent is frequently ignored. Thus, 300 percent of a sum does not treble a given sum: it quadruples it. And so on.

*An Object Cannot be in **Two Places at Once***

But an electron suffering diffraction can. It also seems clear that though size and position is infinitely variable, everything shares the same time; but, as Einstein showed, this is not so. We must check our intuitive ideas all the time.

U V

Swimming is Dangerous
Where There is an **Undertow**

There is no objective 'undertow' in water that is not immediately reversed. An active and persistent seaward underflow at the bottom demands the occurrence of a correspondingly active and persistent shoreward flow at the surface. Except under doubly specialized conditions of wind direction and shore configurations, 'undertow' does not exist and never has, outside the imagination of frightened swimmers. The intermittent seaward pull as each wave slides back from the beach is reversed every few seconds by an equally temporary shoreward movement of the next wave.

Nature Abhors a **Vacuum**

This idea of Aristotle was universally accepted until Torricelli (1608–1647) showed that if a tube closed at one end is filled with mercury and inverted, the mercury will stand up to the top of the tube only if the tube is less than 30 inches long; evidently Nature's abhorrence of a vacuum is limited.

'Viking' Rhymes with 'Liking'

It rhymes on the contrary with 'licking', as *vik* (Icelandic) means 'creek, inlet, or bay', and *ingr* (in Icelandic; in Anglo-Saxon *ing*) means 'people of', or 'belonging to'. The Anglo-Saxon word *wicing* is therefore a borrowing from Scandinavia.

If it is argued that long incorrect usage makes the incorrect into the correct, it should be remembered that a language as far removed from Scandinavian as Italian has always employed the correct pronunciation in *vichingo*. The correct pronunciation appears in the Scottish coastal town of Wick, and all such compounds as Ler*wick*.

W

Washington Cut Down a Cherry Tree
Belonging to His Father

Mason L. Weems' biography of George Washington relates the now-celebrated story that the boy cut down a cherry tree belonging to his father and, when asked if he had done it, admitted the deed, adding "I cannot tell a lie". Despite the fact that Weems' fabrication of this entirely apocryphal incident was exposed shortly after its publication, Newnes' *Pictorial Knowledge* (vol. 2, London, 1947, p. 159) repeats that "George Washington is known as 'The boy who could not tell a lie' . . .", and countless children repeat the fairytale as fact. Another error is to think of the boy Washington as a pacifist. On the contrary, he was praised as 'first in war and first in peace' after a successful military and political career.

"Elementary, My Dear **Watson!**"

I may be blind, forgetful, or merely careless, but I have read all the Sherlock Holmes stories of Sir Arthur Conan Doyle, and cannot remember ever having come across on one single occasion the phrase which is allegedly characteristic of the great detective. It crops up, though not as a quotation, on page 100 of Hesketh Pearson's *Conan Doyle: his life and art* (London, 1946), but not—so far as I know—in the works of Doyle himself. Can any reader prove the contrary?

Watt Invented the Steam Engine

James Watt (1736–1819) is the familiar hero of the tale you heard at your mother's knee: holding an egg-cup in steam from the spout of a kettle, he saw the steam condense on it, scalded his fingers, dropped the egg-cup which caused it to break and his granny to scold him for his idle daydreaming.

The steam engine was apparently first designed by Edward Somerset, Marquis and Earl of Worcester in 1655 and patented by Robert Hooke in 1678. The pumping steam engine was invented by Sir Samuel Morland in 1682. A model pumping steam engine was first exhibited by Denis Papin in 1685. Still before Watt's birth, Thomas Newcomen erected the first practical working steam engine at Tipton, Staffordshire, in 1712. Watt's achievement was a great improvement in efficiency by condensing the steam in a separate closed vessel instead of in the cylinder itself; he also closed the top of the cylinder and used low-pressure steam instead of cold air to drive the piston down.

Welsh Rarebit Is a Corruption of Welsh Rabbit

Welsh rabbit is toasted cheese. Skeat dealt with the above fallacy in his *Etymological dictionary* by pointing out that those who were too dense to see the joke of calling toasted cheese 'Welsh rabbit' pretended that the name is a corruption of 'Welsh rarebit', "which is as pointless and stupid as it is incapable of proof".

It may have arisen because the original jokers thought that there were no rabbits in Wales, because in Australia there was a dish called 'colonial goose' (mutton cooked with stuffing) from the times before geese were introduced there. Similar nonsense names used in cooking include 'Irish apricots' or 'Munster plums' for potatoes; 'Gravesend sweetmeats' for shrimps; 'Essex lion' for veal; 'Glasgow magistrates' for herrings; and 'Fieldlane duck' for baked sheep's head.

Whales Spout Water Through Their Blow-Holes

Whales breathe through their lungs and, being unable to separate air from water as fishes do, must rise to the surface to breathe. The 'spouting' of the whale, which is commonly mistaken at a (safe) distance for water, is in fact the ordinary act of breathing out that any mammal has to perform, but in the case of the whale the intervals between breathing out are longer and the action therefore seems to be more dramatic. If the breathing out takes place under water of course it is water that is ejected, but this is relatively rarely seen, and the observer usually sees the ejection of air (highly charged with watery vapour) mixed with mucous matter.

A Breed of *White Elephants* Exists

No true white elephant has ever yet been reported, but Dusit Zoo in Bangkok usually exhibits a salmon-pink (albino) elephant, which is sold to the Royal Family when born since 'white' elephants are a rarity even in Asia.

The veneration of the Thais for white elephants is

shown by a marvellous description written by a Siamese ambassador at the Court of Queen Victoria who wished to evoke the respect due to her in the following gallant terms; "One cannot but be struck by the deportment of the revered Queen of England. She clearly comes of a divine line of warrior kings and conquerors of the world. Her eyes, her complexion, and above all her fascination are those of a splendid and majestic White Elephant".

Wolves Hunt in Packs

Not outside the realms of the popular movie or children's adventure story. As Stefansson remarks in *The standardisation of error* (London, 1928), *zoological* wolves go in pairs or families, never above a dozen.

Stefansson tracked down all reports of wolf-packs over a period of twenty years, and not one had been authenticated. Neither is there a single authenticated account of a wolf's having attacked and eaten a human being. This fallacy persisted so strongly that the Biological Survey in Washington carefully checked up on every published account of the killing of human beings by wolves in both the U.S.A. and Canada, and "without a single exception they proved to be purely imaginary". This might not seem so surprising, were it not for the fact that between January and March 1929, the *New York Times Index* showed reports of wolves devouring 16 Austrians, 5 Poles, an aged Bulgarian priest and many Czechoslovaks. They also 'menaced Constantinople', whatever that might mean.

Women's Brains are Smaller than Men's

As a generalization there is some truth in the common belief, but the various qualifications attaching to the statement render it worthless. First, not all women's brains are smaller than all men's. Second, the average woman's body is also smaller than that of the average man. Third, taking into account the proportionate size of the body, the weight of the brain is roughly equal in both sexes. Brain size varies in proportion to body weight, race, stature, and age.

Finally, the size of the brain is related neither to the gender nor to the intelligence of its owner.

XYZ

English Monarchs Have Always Been Addressed As *"Your Majesty"*

The first English monarch whom we know to have been addressed as "Your Majesty" was Henry VIII. The mode of address varied from reign to reign so that, for instance, we have records of "Your Grace" (Henry IV), "Your Excellent Grace" (Henry VI), and "High and Mighty Prince" (Edward IV).

Zoological Fallacies

That inbreeding causes degeneration (it causes the intensification of known characteristics); that ants and bees are intelligent; that certain fly larvae, living as guests in ants' nests, are molluscs; that selection can gradually change the nature of an hereditary factor, or gene; that toads at the breeding season find ponds through an ability to sense water from a distance; and that fishes can sense a current as such and swim against it when unable to see or feel the bank or bottom of the stream . . .

The Last Fallacy

Or perhaps better to say 'the first fallacy'. To assume that, in every single case where I in my ignorance have selected what I have thought the best available advice, there is consequently no room for error. A glance behind my shoulder to similarly assured lists of popular delusions over the centuries is enough to persuade me that more than one of my foregoing assertions is incorrect, and that the reader should consult this book no less than any other with a sceptical air, as if to say "this too may be wrong: let me never trust what is offered as fact, truth, or wisdom without testing it in the light of experience and observation".

APPENDIX
Some Terms and Themes in Fallacious Reasoning

Abiogenesis

The production of living by not-living matter, or 'spontaneous generation'. The term was introduced by Prof. T. H. Huxley in *Brit. Assoc. Rep.* LXXVI, but it is a fallacy repeated many times in the history of pseudoscience. Aristotle taught as a fact that animals spring from putrid matter, and it was not until 1668 that the Italian Redi conclusively proved that no maggots were 'bred' in meat on which flies were prevented by wire screens from laying their eggs.

Pasteur refuted abiogenesis in the microscopic world, and it is now generally agreed (except by theosophists and some other sectarians) that all known living organisms rise only from preexisting living organisms. However, Huxley refuted only contemporary abiogenesis, noting that there was probably once a primordial archebiosis which remains unknown; in other words, in the remote past protoplasm may have developed from non-living matter by a series of steps which are not yet understood, and may possibly never be understood.

Among the well-known abiogenetic fallacies are those of Andrew Crosse, an Englishman who claimed in 1836 to have produced living creatures by passing an electrical current through certain chemical mixtures; of John Butler Burke, whose book *The origin of life* (1906) created wild interest because of its claim that the author had produced primitive artificial forms half living and half crystalline; and of a third Englishman, Morley Martin, who died in 1937 after claiming to produce from the fossil-free Azoic rock what he described as 'primordial protoplasm'.

The 'Chicken Before the Egg' Fallacy, or the Error of **Absolute Priority**

It is not true that there must be an absolute first term in any causal series, and that if event A_1 can be said to cause event B_1, the same cannot be said of B_1 and A_2.

American historians, for instance, have traditionally oversimplified the problem of causality between the observable cultural (not *racial*) inferiority of American negroes and prejudice against negroes.

Gunnar Myrdal has persuasively argued that there was a vicious circle, in which intense anti-negro cultural prejudice from the very beginning of modern American history was a contributing factor in the situation, but others no less potent included the nature of an African negro's cultural heritage, the nature of Anglo-American culture, and the nature of the acculturative process. These factors placed the negro in a position of cultural inferiority from the very start.

Amphiboly

A linguistic fallacy due to double meanings of words, or phrases or sentences including words with double meanings.

Abraham Fraunce, in *The lawiers logike, exemplifying the praecepts of logike by the practise of the common lawe* (London, 1588) defined amphiboly as any case "when the sentence may be turned both the wayes, so that a man shall be uncertayne what waye to take, . . . as that olde sophister the Devill deluded *Pyrrhus* by giving him such an intricate answere: *Aio te, Aeacida, Romanos vincere posse*".

The Latin sentence can be construed both 'I say that the Romans can conquer you' and 'I say that you can conquer the Romans', Aeacida referring to King Pyrrhus. (This cunning use of the Latin accusative-and-infinitive construction also helps to demonstrate the fallaciousness of a Latin teacher's argument that the correct application of case-endings will wholly prevent ambiguity in a Latin text).

Note further that Fraunce's example is doubly ambiguous by the use of *posse* ('can'), implying that the prediction is equally true if either of the eventualities cunningly prophesied *fail* to occur.

However, I prefer the wartime austerity slogan offered by Irving Copi, in his *Introduction to logic* (2nd ed., New York, 1961) to illustrate amphiboly: SAVE SOAP AND WASTE PAPER.

Inheritance of Acquired **Characteristics**

A major zoological error, which persisted among many zoologists well into the 20th century, was the Lamarckian belief in the inheritance of acquired characteristics: the hypothesis that bodily or somatic changes experienced by the individual as a result of either environmental influences or his own activities would somehow be passed on to his offspring and reappear in some measure in the absence of similar influences and activities.

The theory lost impetus with the work of August Weismann (1834–1914), who advanced a view of the continuing germ-plasm as distinct from the somatoplasm, making it clear that germ-cells form a continuous line, not only between generations but also through the body of the individual in each generation.

174

Squaring the **Circle**

Montucla's *Histoire des récherches sur la quadrature du cercle* (Paris, 1754; 2nd ed., 1831) and Augustus de Morgan's *Budget of paradoxes* (London, 1872) are full of accounts of pseudo-mathematicians who have obtained by illegitimate means a Euclidean construction for the quadrature of the circle, or a finitely expressible value for π, and proceeded to use faulty reasoning and/or defective mathematics to establish their assertions.

When the squaring of the circle is spoken of, it is assumed that the restrictions of Euclidean geometry apply. The problem is so ancient, and has been tackled by so many leading mathematicians of every generation, that every claim to have solved it must, tentatively at least, be considered fallacious.

Circular 'Proof'

Or *petitio principii* (Latin, 'begging the question'). This is a very common error, and can be exemplified by a statement of the theologian Barth: "That revelation is revelation can be known only by revelation" to justify his own beliefs. But the statement justifies nothing at all.

Less obviously fallacious reasoning occurs in Michael Walzer's *The revolution of the saints* (Cambridge, 1965). It is hoped to demonstrate, by an appeal to historical evidence, that a certain complex of ideas attached to Puritanism. But when Walzer discovers these ideas, he assumes that the thought of the man who expresses them is 'Puritanical' simply because he expresses them. Briefly, he assumes that Puritans were men who thought the 'XYZ' galaxy of ideas, and then proves the thesis by assuming that men who thought 'XYZ' were Puritanical.

The opposite fallacy is equally bad: that of treating an advanced proposition as a begging of the question as soon as one sees that, if established, it would establish the question.

Arnold Toynbee (in vol. 9 of *A study of history*, p. 196) wrote: "We may perhaps take it as having been already demonstrated that an historian's professed inability to discern any plot, rhythm, or predetermined pattern is no evidence that blind Samson has actually won his boasted freedom from the bondage of the 'Laws of Nature'. The presumption is indeed the opposite; for, when bonds are imperceptible to the wearer of them, they are likely to prove more difficult to shake off than when they betray their presence and reveal something of their shape and texture by clanking and galling".

In *The use of reason* (London, 1960, p. 226), E. R. Emmet argues that this is supposed to mean "Invisible bonds are hard to shake off; X cannot see any bonds; Therefore they are hard to shake off; Therefore the presumption is that they are still there".

Cycles of History

Giambattista Vico (1668–1744) is only one of the millions of people, learned and lay alike, whose concept of the world they live in has been hopelessly confused by the fallacy that 'this kind of thing happens every hundred years'. Vico made a false analogy between the life of a human being and the course of a civilization. He argued that a man or woman, in the course of a lifetime, passes through phases of feeling, imagination and thinking. In the same way, a civilization passes through ages of gods, heroes, and humanity. A purely bestial phase passes into a primitive period, then to an intellectual and spiritual period, and finally to an era of humanity. The 'energies' of the civilization then fade and die away, to be followed by another primitive phase. The problem with this world-view is that it is entirely fallacious as a *principle*, even if it can be made into a Procrustean bed that certain civilizations can be stretched to fit. In what sense, for instance, does the great and enduring civilization of China correspond in phases to the civilizations of the Congo pygmies or the Indians of the Canadian plains? Similar cyclical theories, attractive in their simplicity but wholly useless as tools for the understanding of the course of human societies, have been propagated by Oswald Spengler and Arnold Toynbee, but their *principles* are no more scientific than those of Vico's *Principi di una scienza nuova intorno alla natura delle nazioni* (Naples, 1725).

Stebbing on the **Definition** of Fallacies

"The word 'fallacy' has unfortunately often been used in different senses", writes L. Susan Stebbing in *Thinking to some purpose* (Harmondsworth, 1939, pp. 156–7). "It is used sometimes as a synonym for 'error of fact', as in the statement: 'It is a fallacy to suppose that aeroplanes can be built by mass-production'. This is, in my opinion, a plainly erroneous use of the word. The speaker meant that aeroplanes cannot, in fact, be produced by methods suitable to the production of, say, motor-cars. I shall assume, without further dis-

177

cussion that the speaker, in using 'fallacy' in this sense, was simply showing his ignorance of the correct usage of the word. There remains to be noticed an ambiguity that is more important for our present purpose. If we say: "He is guilty of a fallacy", we sometimes mean to imply that he is guilty of a deception. The *Shorter Oxford English Dictionary* gives as a meaning of 'fallacy', now obsolete, 'deception', 'trickery'. This obsolete meaning does, I think, influence our modern usage. It would certainly be an advantage if we recognized that to accuse a person of having committed a fallacy is not to accuse him of intent to deceive. A fallacy is a violation of a logical principle; 'to fall into a fallacy' is to slip into 'an unsound form of argument', that is, to make a mistake *in reasoning*, not in what is *reasoned about*. If we mistakenly suppose that we have premises adequate to establish our conclusion, then we are reasoning illogically and thus committing a fallacy.

If we think of a fallacy as a deception, we are too likely to take it for granted that we need to be cautious in looking out for fallacies only when other people are arguing with us. We come to suppose that a fallacy is a trick and, thus, as involving deliberate dishonesty. Thinking along these lines, we are apt to assume that where there is no dispute, and so no disputant, there is no danger of fallacies, so that honesty of intention will suffice to keep our reasoning sound. This is a profound mistake".

Etymological Fallacies

In the words of A. Smythe Palmer—and every philologist would quickly endorse them—"there are a multitude of words which have been either altered from their true form or perverted from their proper meaning owing to popular mistakes or misunderstandings as to their derivation or kinship to other words". The *Oxford English Dictionary*, Skeat's *Etymological dictionary* and Partridge's *Origins* (4th ed., 1966) are primary reference tools, though perhaps too voluminous for those interested primarily in errors of etymology. For the latter study one might commend *Folk etymology* (1882) and *The folk and their word-lore* (1904) by A. Smythe Palmer, as regards the English language. He considers the erroneous metamorphosis of foreign words, verbal corruptions, mistaken analogies, and misinterpretations.

Etymology is a science based on the laws of language and demands a historical and comparative knowledge not only of the particular language studied, but also of those related in any relevant manner.

Fanciful sources for names are almost as widespread as they were before etymological dictionaries made them indefensible. Thus, one can still find countrymen who derive the word 'partridge' from the birds' habit of lying between the furrows of ploughed land, and so they part ridges *(Gentleman's Magazine,* February 1892). De Thaun, in his *Livre des créatures,* claimed that the same bird was called 'perdix' because it loses *(pert, perdit)* its brood. Eric Partridge, who ought to know, honestly admits that he doesn't. He merely quotes Hofmann's opinion that the Latin *perdix,* adopted from Greek, might echo the whirring wings of the rising bird.

My own favourite etymological fallacy is connected with the fallacy of the Tower of Babel, and can be found in the *Opera* (Antwerp, 1580) of the 16th-century Flemish scholar Johannes Goropius. On finding that the word 'sack' is similar in many of the lan-

179

guages we have since learned belong to the Indo-European linguistic group (*sakkos* in Greek, *saccus* in Latin, *sacco* in Italian, and *saco* in Spanish, etc.), Goropius concluded that, at the moment of the confusion of language, every single labourer working in the Tower of Babel remembered to carry away his sack.

Holist Fallacies

The holist fallacy is the mistaken idea that a historian should select significant details from a sense of the whole thing. Though plausible at first glance, this would prevent a historian from knowing anything until he knows everything, which is both absurd and impossible.

The weakness of holism is best exemplified by the attack on Hegel's *Philosophy of history* in Bertrand Russell's *History of western philosophy* (London, 1945), pp. 743 and 745.

"The view of Hegel and of many other philosophers", writes Russell, "is that the character of any portion of the universe is so profoundly affected by its relations to the other parts and to the whole, that no true statement can be made about any part except to assign its place in the whole. Thus there can be only one true statement; there is no truth except the whole truth . . . Now this is all very well, but it is open to an initial objection. If the above argument were sound, how could knowledge ever begin? I know numbers of propositions of the form "A is the father of B", but I do not know the whole universe. If all knowledge were knowledge of the universe as a whole there would be no knowledge. This is enough to make us suspect a mistake somewhere".

Hegel's work is so riddled with fallacies that D. H. Fischer, author of *Historians' fallacies* (New York, 1970), states that most of the fallacies in his book could be illustrated by [Hegel's] arguments. "All metahistorians, by definition, are guilty of this mistake—Toynbee, Spengler, Sorokin, Marx, Comte, Kant, Condorcet, Vico—and others who have tried to discover *the* "meaning" of *the* "past".

Charles **Lamb**'s Fallacies

One of the *Last essays of Elia* (London, 1833) is on popular fallacies, which Charles Lamb lists as follows: that a bully is always a coward; that ill-gotten gain never prospers; that a man must not laugh at his own jest; that such a one shows his breeding—that it is easy to perceive he is no gentleman; that the poor copy the vices of the rich; that enough is as good as a feast; that of two disputants the warmer is generally in the wrong; that verbal allusions are not wit, because they will not bear a translation; that the worst puns are the best; that handsome is as handsome does; that we must not look a gift-horse in the mouth; that home is home though it is never so homely; that you must love me and love my dog; that we should rise with the lark; that we should lie down with the lamb; and, that a sulky temper is a misfortune.

Lysenkoism

Trofim D. Lysenko was the Soviet Union's leading authority on heredity and evolution. With Lamarck, the

181

pre-Darwinian French scientist, Lysenko believed that evolution worked through the inheritance of traits which organisms acquired in response to their surroundings, as in the case of the giraffe's long neck. Giraffes stretched their necks to eat leaves which were beyond the reach of lesser animals, and because this trait was effective, giraffes with longer and longer necks were born. Darwin accepted this fact, but suggested that it was more important that the giraffes with shorter necks died out, thus proving the survival of the fittest. Evolution theory (q.v.) has now rejected Lamarckianism, but it was official party policy in the USSR and in two articles on Lysenkoism for the *Saturday Review* (4 and 11 December 1948), the Nobel Prize-winning geneticist H. J. Muller described what had happened to Lysenko's opponents: "In 1933 or thereabouts, the geneticists Chetverikoff, Ferry, and Ephroimson were all, on separate occasions, banished to Siberia, and Levitsky to a labor camp in the European Arctic . . . from 1936 on Soviet geneticists of all ranks lived a life of terror . . . Ironically, the great majority of the geneticists who have been purged were thoroughly loyal politically; many were even ardent crusaders for the Soviet system and leadership as the writer well knows through personal contact with them".

Muller continues to explain that the Lysenkoist view "implies a mystical Aristotelian 'perfecting principle', a kind of foresight, in the basic make-up of living things, despite the fact that it claims in the same breath not to be 'idealistic' at all".

Mathematical Fallacies

Dr E. A. Maxwell of Queens' College, Cambridge, has written a useful (if brief) introduction: *Fallacies in mathematics* (Cambridge, 1959) in which he explains that a mathematical fallacy "leads by guile to a wrong but plausible conclusion", whereas a mistake is an error of little consequence and a howler denotes an error which leads innocently to a correct result. Dr Maxwell devotes his final chapter to howlers, no space at all to mistakes, and ten chapters to fallacies. Among the geometrical fallacies are: "To prove that every triangle is isosceles"; "To prove that every angle is a right angle"; "To prove that, if ABCD is a quadrilateral in which AB = CD, then AD is necessarily parallel to BC"; and "To prove that every point inside a circle lies on its circumference".

The algebraic and trigonometrical fallacies include: "That $4 = 0$"; "That $+1 = -1$"; "That all lengths are equal"; and "That the sum of the squares on two sides of a triangle is never less than the square on the third".

Dr Maxwell also disposes of the fallacies that $0 = 1$; that $2 = 1$; that $\pi = 0$; that a cycloid has arches of zero length; and some 'limit' fallacies.

Mathematical Truths Can be Completely Proved Within the System

Kurt Gödel, in an epoch-making paper published in 1931, showed that the deductive system of A. N. Whitehead and Bertrand Russell's *Principia mathematica* (Cambridge, 1910–13), and also related systems such as standard set theory, contain 'undecidable' statements, which may be defined as statements that *are* true within the system but cannot be proved to be true *within* the system. More precisely, Gödel demonstrates that if a system (like that of *Principia mathematica*) satisfies certain reasonable conditions such as consistency (defined as 'freedom from contradiction'), then it allows the formation of sentences that are undecidable. Gödel also shows that, if such a system is consistent, there is no way to prove that consistency within the system. In a certain sense, therefore, mathematical truth cannot be completely proved.

However, as E. Nagel and J. R. Newman stress in their *Gödel's proof* (London, 1959, p. 101), "Gödel's proof should not be construed as an invitation to despair or as an excuse for mystery-mongering. The discovery that there are arithmetical truths which cannot be demonstrated formally does not mean that there are truths which are forever incapable of becoming known, or that a 'mystic' intuition (radically different in kind and authority from what is generally operative in intellectual advances) must replace cogent proof. It does not mean, as a recent writer claims, that there are 'ineluctable limits to human reason'. It does mean that the resources of the human intellect have not been, and cannot be, fully formalized, and the new principles of demonstration forever await invention and discovery".

Mechanistic Fallacies

This group of fallacies has been defined by R. M. MacIver, in *Social causation* (2nd ed., New York, 1964). It

184

treats the various components of a social situation, or of any organized system, as though they were detachable, isolable, homogeneous, independently operative, and therefore susceptible of being added to or subtracted from the causal complex, increasing or decreasing the result-by that amount. But even a slight acquaintance with the mechanism itself should teach us to avoid this fallacy.

Two examples of this fallacy, so prevalent in historical and philosophical writing, are provided by J. B. Bury in his *History of the later Roman Empire* (2 vols., New York, 1958, vol. 1, pp. 308–9) and by the eminent French mediaevalist Marc Bloch in *Feudal society* (Chicago, 1961, pp. 35–8).

Bury eliminated depopulation, the Christian religion, and the fiscal system as causes of the dismemberment of the Roman Empire, stating that a combination of some or all of these could not have been responsible for the Empire's dismemberment by the barbarians in the West since the same causes operated in the East, but there the Empire survived much longer intact and united. But, as Morton White explains in *The foundations of historical knowledge* (New York, 1965), the three causal elements which Bury rejects may have interacted with each other, and with other elements, in such a way as to produce results in the West very different from those in the East.

Bloch considers the cessation of Scandinavian pillaging in the Middle Ages *not* to be explicable by the fact that the Scandinavians were converted to Christianity, noting the false generalization that no Christian people would indulge in pillaging: "there was apparently no difficulty in reconciling ardent faith in the Christian mysteries with a taste for violence and plunder, nay even with the most conscious glorification of war". Yet when Bloch tries to explain the beginning of the Scandinavian invasions, he accepts the explanation that the Scandinavian countries were overpopulated at the time. However, he would deny, surely, that the people of every overpopulated country invade in the manner of the mediaeval Scandinavians.

Nature Has 'Laws'

The 'laws of nature' are observed and recorded by men, and thus as clearly man-made as penal or commercial laws. They, like penal or commercial laws, must also be modified in the light of changing circumstances to conform to new facts.

Julian Huxley wrote in his *Essays of a biologist* (1923): "A law of Nature is not (and I wonder how often this fallacy has been exploded, only to reappear next day)—a law of Nature is not something revealed, not something absolute, nor something imposed on phenomena from without or from above; it is no more and no less than a summing-up in generalised form, of our own observations of phenomena; it is an epitome of fact, from which we can draw general conclusions".

I would add only this: where agreed 'laws of nature' are attacked explicitly or implicitly by those writers whose ideas are generically termed 'fallacies' throughout this book, the onus is clearly upon them to prove that the 'laws of nature' have been changed (and to show where and how). The onus is not upon those who accept the current but perennially-mutating 'laws of nature' to show why they do so.

Top Hat Fallacy

The celebrated 'Top Hat Fallacy' has been restated by Conrad Waddington in *Tools for thought* (London, 1977, p. 139):

"It is important to realize what a correlation between two variables means and, in particular, what it does *not* mean. It means that, in the population studied *(not* necessarily in all populations), there is a tendency, whose strength is expressed in the correlation coefficient, for the measurements of the two correlated characteristics on the same individual (say, its height and weight) to vary together; the more one measurement departs from the average, the more the other will do so too. This does *not* mean that one characteristic causes the other; it may do so, but the fact that they are correlated is not good evidence to reach that conclusion. They can both be caused by something else, and have no essential causal relation to each other. This is a very basic point of warning about the misuse of statistics. It is usually enshrined in an old parable, known as the 'Top Hat Fallacy'—and the fact that it is out of date sartorially should not make you forget that it is still bang-on in what it implies. I quote it in the words of a former President of the Royal Society, in his memorandum about how to do operational research: 'Statistical investigation of the population of many cities would show that the wearers of top hats are significantly taller than the average. The missing causally effective variable here is clearly the higher average income of the top-hat-wearing group' ".

Browne on Vulgar **Errors**

Sir Thomas Browne, the great English stylist of *Religio medici* (authorized ed., 1643) and *Hydrotaphia* (1658), is to be credited with the first attempt at a comprehensive survey of vulgar errors (as opposed to a classification of them) in *Pseudodoxia epidemica: or, enquiries into very many received tenents, and commonly presumed truths* (London, 1646), a book usually referred to as *Vulgar errors*.

Pseudodoxia epidemica is divided into seven books, the most interesting being the first, which is introductory. This deals with the fallibility of human nature as a source of fallacies, including credulity, false deduction, supinity, adherence to antiquity, tradition and authority. Browne considered himself absolutely free from heretical opinions as a Christian (the *Religio medici* appeared in Paris, where he was thought a Roman Catholic), but the Vatican placed the work on the *Index Expurgatorius* to be on the safe side. Browne gives a list of those authors to be treated with caution. Among them is Pliny, whose *Historia naturalis* is condemned in words that really demand to be reproduced: "there is scarce a popular errour passant in our dayes, which is not either directly expressed, or diductively contained in this worke, which being in the hands of most men, hath proved a powerfull occasion of their propogation . . ." It is worth mentioning, for those readers sceptical of Browne's wholesale disapproval, that Howard M. Parshley echoes Browne's view in *The story of human error* (New York, 1936) edited by Joseph Jastrow: "Pliny's *Historia naturalis* was so stuffed with errors of the time that it undoubtedly takes the palm as the greatest single repository of misinformation known to man".

Book two of Browne's work is devoted to errors concerning minerals and vegetables; book three is on animals; book four on man; book five is on "many things questionable as they are described in pictures" and on various superstitions; book six on geographical and historical fallacies; and book seven on religious errors, and a pot-pourri of such picturesque errors as those "that the Army of Xerxes drank whole rivers dry" and "of the wandring Iew".

Like all writers on fallacies, Browne knew that he was fallible, and added a caveat in his preface that "we are not Magisteriall in opinions, nor have wee Dictator-like obtruded our conceptions, but in the humility of Enquiries or disquisitions, have only proposed them unto more ocular discerners". Again like all writers on fallacies including myself and beyond, he was credulous about some beliefs which later ages exposed as fallacious and, to his discredit, gave testimony at Norwich in 1664 which led to the death of two 'witches', the wretched Amy Duny and Rose Cullender.

Fovargue on *Vulgar Errors*

Stephen Fovargue's *A new catalogue of vulgar errors* (Cambridge, 1767) is a collection of thirty-six essays, some of them discursive and a few even digressive, which indicate some of the commonest fallacies of the mid-18th century in England. I append a complete list of Fovargue's fallacies.

1. That the more ammunition is put into a fowling piece, the farther it will do execution.
2. That the heron makes a hole in the bottom of her

189

nest, through which her feet hang, when she sits upon her eggs.

3. That the bittern puts his bill or beak into a reed, and that the reed gives, by the breath and motion of the beak of the bird, that deep and low note which we so frequently hear him make as he lies in a Fenn.

4. That the tone of a violin is to be brought out, by laying on like a blacksmith.

5. That the farther you go south, the hotter is the climate.

6. That exactly under the Aequator is always the hottest climate on the globe.

7. That the more hay is dried in the sun, the better it will be.

8. That the violin is a wanton instrument, and not proper for psalms; and that the organ is not proper for country-dances, and brisk airs.

9. That the Organ and Harpsichord are the two principal instruments, and that other instruments are inferior to them in a concert.

10. That every key in music ought to have a different effect or sound.

11. That a piece of music which has flats set before it, is in a flat key on that account, and vice versa with sharps.

12. That apparitions or spectres do exist, or that the ghosts of men do appear at, before, or after their deaths.

13. That bleeding is proper for a patient, who is apt to be sick in a morning. [On scurvy.]

14. That no thing which moves upon the surface of the earth, is so swift as the wind. ["Even pigeons and swallows can go faster".]

15. That there is now, or ever was, such a science as astrology. [Fovargue would be astonished to find this error still widespread two centuries later.]

16. Most Londoners are mistaken when they think that they have wit enough to impose on countrymen. [Wrongly phrased; Fovargue does *not* think this a fallacy; he himself was a Fenman.]

17. That a pointer, if he lifts up his foot, when he comes upon game, does it in order to shew his master the spot where the birds lie. [It is coincidental.]

18. That the way to make boys learn their books, is to keep them in school all day, and whip them.

19. That clogging their parts with long grammar rules, will make them bright scholars.

20. That teaching boys Bawdy Books will make them religious men and good clergymen. [The 'Bawdy Books' are by that 'Master of Intrigue' Ovid and that 'Libertine' Horace.]

21. That the present age is a duller Age, and less ingenious, than those which are past.

22. That the musical composition of this present age is inferior to that of the last.

23. That the hearing of musical performances, is apt to soften men too much, and by that means to give them an effeminate manner.

24. That the Italian operas consist of effeminate musick.

25. That nothing is poetry but what is wrote in rhyme.

26. That kicking up the heel behind, and twisting round upon one leg, is fine scating.

27. That using hard words and long sentences, in discourse or in writing, is an indication of scholarship.

28. That the way to get a sailing boat off the shore, when she is fast by any accident, is to let go both or all the sails, and stand at her head, and push with a sprit.

29. That planting aquatics upon banks of the Fenns will preserve and strengthen them, so as to render them more able to resist the force of a flood.

191

30. That those who lived 2000 years ago, were larger than the present race of mankind.

31. That bleeding in May will preserve the constitution against illness during the ensuing summer.

32. That negroes are not a part of the human species. [Refutes with the aid of Locke's *Essay concerning human understanding*].

33. That negroes are the descendants of Cain, and that the colour of their skins is that mark which was set upon Cain, after killing Abel.

34. That Love is nothing but concupiscence to a high degree, or that love and lust are the same thing.

35. That the Hedge-Hog is a mischievous animal; and particularly that he sucks cows, when they are asleep in the night, and causes their teats to be sore.

36. That a person is the better or the worse for being of any particular calling or profession.